BUBBLE, BUBBLE, TOIL AND TROUBLE

BUBBLE, BUBBLE, TOIL AND TROUBLE

Shirley Lueth

WILLIAM MORROW AND COMPANY, INC.

New York   1984

Library of Congress Catalog Card Number: 83-63299

ISBN: 0-688-03112-9

Printed in the United States of America

First Edition

1 2 3 4 5 6 7 8 9 10

BOOK DESIGN BY BERNARD SCHLEIFER

To my best friend . . . Lee
To all my children
To Diane Cleaver . . . she kept the faith
To Page Cuddy . . . an editor with a smile in her heart
And to those good neighbors and friends who share these memories
I love you all.

FOREWORD

NEIGHBORS AND FRIENDS have always been important
to me. I can honestly say I doubt that I could've survived
even one year of raising our seven children without
them. I borrowed their eggs, card tables, best dishes,
and their shoulders to cry on. I called them on the telephone for recipes, advice on colic, to warn them the Ful-
ler Brush man was in the neighborhood, and to hear a
voice that could say something in complete sentences.
Not once did any of our neighbors call me Mom or ask
for money. We shared school report cards, daydreams,
birth announcements, car pools, coffee cake, and each
other's children. We didn't share each other's lipstick,
underwear, or husbands. We were close but we weren't
that close. Once in a while I even peeked into their windows so I could write this book.

Three hundred sixty-five days can be a long time
when you're restricted to a split-level house that con-
tains a husband who never throws anything away, five
daughters who sincerely want to be movie stars, two
sons who think they might eventually like to be gangsters, and a dog who lives each day as though he'd died
and gone to heaven. Augie-Doggie was the star of the
show and proved it by dropping his dog dish on my foot
whenever he got the chance.

7

"Can you imagine," I told my neighbor Helen, one day when we were sharing strong coffee and a stale roll, "what my life would've been like had I produced only one perfect, intelligent, clever, and beautiful child instead of seven?" I wasn't bragging, mind you, only telling a mother's truth.

Helen snorted and looked over the rim of her coffee cup at our humble kitchen. There wasn't a countertop in sight that wasn't tiled in crumbs. "Possibly you would've been better organized," she observed. Helen felt being unorganized was the same as committing a major sin. She also felt this way about gluttony, lust, slothfulness, and plastic tablecloths. She was positive I was bound for hell with a ticker tape of undone earthly chores wrapped around my neck and she was probably right, but I was too busy to worry about it. Helen had three well-spaced children and during her pregnancies looked as if she might have swallowed an avocado seed. She also had a mannerly dog and cat that didn't scratch the front door or build litter boxes in the backyard. Her husband, Ray, wasn't allowed to smoke a cigar in their house except on holidays or when I had a baby. Ray became my protector and was the only one on the block who didn't titter behind my back or suggest I look up Family Planning seminars in the Yellow Pages. He was as excited about my pregnancies as I was.

When Amy was born the day after Christmas, dear Ray became so wrought up over the miracle of being permitted *two* whole cigars within a forty-eight-hour period, he had heart palpitations and spent a lot of money on specialists to determine if he had long to live. I'm not sure he ever forgave me when I announced to the world (and my husband, Lee) that this daughter would be our last. She wasn't, by the way, much to Ray's delight, Helen's disgust, and Lee's surprise.

Our neighbors became used to seeing me peel out of

our front door, whip down the driveway, and plunge underneath the lilac bushes to retrieve the morning paper while still wearing my nightgown. They were tactful and if they discussed it behind my back I wasn't aware of it. I didn't talk about them either. Oh, once in a while I made an observation, but this wasn't gossiping . . . just simple conversation. "Ray and Helen are getting new drapes in the dining room," I said quietly to my husband. "They've only had them three years. We've had ours nine."

"Nothing wrong with our drapes," Lee said, reaching over to remove a nest of dried Jell-O from the fading fringe. "These are perfectly good drapes. I haven't noticed anything wrong with Ray and Helen's either."

"Helen says they smell like cigar smoke."

"To Helen *everything* smells like cigar smoke." End of discussion and end of my getting new drapes for the dining room.

Lee was an accountant by profession and a Great White Golfer by dreams. He was the type of husband and father who got up in the middle of the night to go to the bathroom, hauled soaking dirty diapers from the toilet bowl, and didn't come in and punch out the one who'd put them there. "Look before you leak!" I warned him over and over. Fortunately for me, Lee always seemed completely happy with his wife, his children, and his home. Comparison to the neighbors wasn't motivation enough for him to rush out and spend money to change his life-style.

I didn't exactly covet my neighbors' possessions but I often gazed wistfully across the street and wondered why their houses looked like models and ours looked maimed. I guess I'd always lived with the "grass is always greener" feeling in the pit of my stomach and I often felt inadequate and so unqualified. One neighbor could sew beautifully, another could sing, and it seemed

everyone could garden and cook well except me. Helen
was loaded with skills. She could chair every organiza-
tion in town with one hand tied behind her back; she
attended banquets and brunches by the dozens and remained as thin as a post. She served on calling commit-
tees without getting cauliflower ear or losing her
temper; kept a spotless house; canned everything that
didn't move for her family table; made her own clothes;
never sweated under her arms; and, somehow, managed
to do all of this and still find time to see every movie,
every television show, and read every book people
talked about. And she always had time to comb her
hair. I was the only one in our neighborhood who
seemed doomed to remaining misplaced in this structure
of order and strong characters.

"But you have the most children," Lee smiled.

So I did. I guess I could do something well after all.

Karen was our oldest child. I learned on her. When
she was a baby, I sat in a rocking chair with her in one
arm, Dr. Spock in the other, and the Bible at my elbow.
I needed all the help I could get and I called on everyone. Quite often it was a contest to see which of us could
cry the loudest and the longest—quite often I won! At
fifteen, Karen was very capable one minute and completely confused the next. Often referred to by relatives
and friends as the oldest of the Lueth Litter, she took
this uncommonly well; though she did accept her first
proposal of marriage at the age of four. After that, she
averaged three or four a year, which kept her father in a
state of constant agitation and her mother at the sewing
machine trying to make gossamer party dresses out of
cheap double knit. Karen learned to cook before she was
twelve and developed a marvelous sense of leadership
that included herding brothers and sisters into a corner
and threatening them with her fist. She also kept a sup-

ply of candy and small toys to slip under their pillows as they slept at night.

Susan at fourteen was our happiness girl. Her concession to growing up was wearing mascara while playing with her Barbie dolls. She had a smile and a temper to match—both broke out when you least expected them. A quarrel was forgiven fifteen minutes after it was over. Although she hardly ever had time to make her bed or clean her room, she always seemed to find a minute or two to flit about the neighborhood confiding in anyone who cared to listen that her mother sometimes forgot her good Christian upbringing early in the morning when the toast burned.

At twelve, John was beginning to swagger when he walked. He resisted homegrown haircuts, kisses from his mother, and changing his underwear. His major ambition at this age was to ride a motorcycle cross country and/or stay out past midnight. He had many friends, none of them girls, and spent most of his evenings playing rousing games of kick-the-can on our denuded front lawn after the vapor lights came on. John could spike a temperature of 104 degrees at will and often played sick when he was quite well. He was our first son and we couldn't have asked for better.

David was ten and because I'd spent so much time on him I decided to keep him. He poked into garbage cans, Dad's tool chest, family secrets, and his teachers' hearts. Physically able to lick his weight in wildcats and mothers, David walked the tightrope of parental finger shaking every day of his young life. He had a dazzling smile, a mania for mischief, spent much of his time standing on his head, and had the enviable ability to see whales where only minnows swam.

Seven-year-old Mary was our fairy child. She lived in a curly haired world of Rose Reds and Snow Whites, waiting for the day when a charming prince would sweep her away from the untidiness of her real-world existence. She shared a room and her toys with Amy, who in five short years had managed to rearrange or carry away everything that wasn't bolted down. Most of the loot was stored and hidden in her side of the closet, which also housed Amy's pretend friends Jane and Betty. Amy always seemed to like kittens better than she did people.

Claudia was our baby, and she was three. She had a miserable temper and often bit important people, but we loved her very much. We still do. In fact, we loved them all, their father and I, but a year is forever when you have only one bathroom and nine people sharing it.

CONTENTS

1

I Didn't Think That Lovers Made Messes

IT WAS A FINE Nebraska spring day. As I poured a second cup of hot tea and contemplated a ladybug drifting across the kitchen cabinets, it occurred to me that I might be accomplishing motherly miracles. True, the floors needed scrubbing, the woodwork looked punished, a sad stove sat hunched in the corner wondering when I was going to abuse it, there wasn't any expensive crystal in evidence, and the wallpaper wasn't flocked. A tipsy ceramic cookie-jar owl winked at me from across the room, and a climbing ivy sat solidly in its dirt, refusing to climb.

Three-year-old Claudia was taking a nap and five-year-old Amy, home from kindergarten, was sitting in the middle of the living room shredding a magazine into confetti to throw on her father when he came home from work. Amy often had little surprises like this ready for her daddy. "It makes life interesting," Lee said, turning his back on wealth and accepting the love of his family as a reasonable substitute. He was a good sport and also a good father. The remaining five children were in school. This is why I had time to drink two cups of tea in one afternoon. When all seven were home I seldom had time to get the tea bag damp, let alone steeped.

I hadn't planned on having seven children. I don't

think anyone does. Thinking back on it, no one had promised me that marriage and motherhood would be easy either. And they were right. They weren't easy. I had gone into marriage with my eyes wide open, with a gentle shove from my mother. Because I was the youngest of four daughters, she no longer grew starry-eyed at the mention of bridal gowns. Mama and I didn't have the usual mother-daughter talk in the secret confines of my bedroom as she adjusted my veil before the ceremony. In fact, I didn't even have a veil. Mama didn't tell me that I'd spend the next million years down on my hands and knees searching for a tax receipt and/or pacifier under the refrigerator or trying to find my meat thermometer in the toy box or listening for teenagers to come home instead of sleeping. She skimmed over these things, bless her heart, patted me on the arm, and wished me luck. My dad, on the other hand, shook my new husband's hand and laughed out loud. Somewhere, somehow, I think he might still be laughing.

It really wasn't anyone's fault that I was an idealistic and impressionable child of the Depression years. I devoured romantic novels during my teen years and memorized the fact that the characters in books never, never woke up to gooey garbage. I honestly didn't think that lovers made messes; and, because sensuous plots didn't cover cleaning up the kitchen before bedtime, I didn't do anything about the kitchen either when I was a newlywed. Imagine my surprise (and my husband's) when I woke up as a bride and discovered the good fairies hadn't tidied up the sink in the night.

"I don't have a clean cup," my groom growled as he prowled through the debris in our honeymoon kitchenette.

"Why do you need a cup?" I asked, peering into the mirror to see if I'd changed in looks now that I was married.

"For my coffee."

"What coffee?" The rotten fairies had let me down again. Putting on the coffeepot, Lee explained that since it was probably going to be up to him to make the money in our family, it was probably going to be up to me to make the meals.

Unfortunately, I didn't know how to cook and it hadn't seemed to matter, because Lee hadn't asked me a thing about cooking when we parked for hours in front of my parents' house with the heater on and the windows cracked to avoid asphyxiation; I certainly wasn't foolish enough to bring up the subject. I knew he'd eventually discover it and I was right about that, because during the first year of our marriage it took me three solid hours of hard work and frustration to prepare a simple salad, green beans, and a meat loaf. I sat curled up in a chair munching red apples and poring over recipes, not understanding a single word in my shiny new cookbooks. Oh, how I longed for the days when all I had to look up in the dictionary was erotic and anatomical terms. Tears and apple juice dripped on the pages as I tried to decipher *parboil, blanch,* and *scorch.* I did quite well with *scorch.* I scorched everything in sight. Sometimes I downright burned it. Or it wasn't cooked at all and remained raw and bleeding.

"You aren't measuring the heat of the stove correctly," Lee said patiently. He was growing thinner and thinner.

"It doesn't say one word in this cookbook about measuring heat," I sobbed. "It only talks about entrées and garnishes and polishing the tea service before entertaining." Hell, I didn't even *own* a tea service.

"My mother used to hold her hand over the stove like this," Lee said, walking over to demonstrate. "She claimed it was a foolproof method. If you can pronounce 'Mississippi' once before snatching your hand away it

means hot; say it twice and the temperature is lukewarm; three pronunciations and it's cooling and probably won't cook much." He waved husbandly hands over
the burners and proudly came up with the correct level
of heat each time. When he came home that evening he
found me wrapped in Unguentine and smelling like
burned fur.

"I forgot the word," I admitted sadly. I'd burned the
pork chops, my left hand, and my ego. Shrugging his
shoulders, Lee kissed my ouchies and reassured me he
hadn't married me for my cooking. We went out for
dinner.

We ate out often during our honeymoon days; but
when you have seven children, Eating Out is filed under
things you'd like to do when left a million dollars by an
old uncle. Since we had no rich relatives we ate at home,
and Lee eventually grew accustomed to salty biscuits,
crusty puddings, sweet sauerkraut, sour desserts, and
mediocre main dishes. The children knew no better. In
some areas my cooking became quite good and in others
it remained questionable. To this day, my cakes still
look better in the box than they do on a plate; but I defy
anyone, anywhere to make a better potato salad.

On that spring morning, however, I admitted to myself that I was probably never going to become a gourmet cook but surely being a good mother stood for
something. And although we hadn't sat at an antique
desk and jotted down in our appointment book "Don't
forget to have baby," we were still pleasantly surprised
and very happy they'd arrived. Counting on my fingers
how many of the children had been born on or near a
holiday, it was obvious our reproductive systems peaked
at the red-letter days on the calendar and took on a real
zip nine months prior to the celebration. We nearly hit
New Year's Day, Christmas, and Halloween, but Easter
was the favorite, as four of the children were born in the
spring.

"It's those rabbit jokes people tell behind our backs," I told Lee. "They've influenced our lives. We're becoming an Easter tradition."

"Why can't we just hide colored eggs like everyone else," he grinned. Thank God, he could still smile. Few husbands coming home from a hard day's work to face a living room that looked like a litter of puppies had just been born in the middle of the rug kept their sense of humor . . . or kept their wives, for that matter. When I said "Guess what?" Lee didn't speculate, he hurried to check the maternity clause in our insurance policy. So, while others sat back quietly and optimistically and waited for Mrs. Spring to wear white clouds on her head and daffodils on her feet, I packed my bag to go to the hospital to have a baby.

The first time was an exciting and thrilling experience. I was ready six months in advance. For days I added to my suitcase—a little lotion here, a new novel there, some stationery, a pretty bed jacket, fancy slippers, and a bottle of do-it-in-bed shampoo. My cosmetic bag bulged with night creams and colognes.

"Why are you taking so much stuff?" Lee wondered as he watched my scurrying about the house in fat, butterball movements. "This baby will think it has rich parents. It won't even want to work its way through college." I told him I wanted our baby's first glimpse of its mother to be memorable. "And I'll need a few things after I get settled in, too," I continued, buffing my nails and spreading proud hands over my lumpy stomach. "I'll need cute pink or blue baby announcements, a camera, some candy for the nurses, my knitting, and the little porcelain angel that sits on our coffee table. I'll also need the family photo albums, seed catalogues, telephone book, and as many newspapers as you can get your hands on."

Lee looked up from his note pad where he'd been busy scribbling my instructions and asked why in the

world I'd need more than one newspaper. "I'm not going
to read them, silly," I said. "I'm going to lay them about
on the bed while I paint." Gathering my watercolors together, I cleaned out my camel's-hair brushes and
placed them carefully in a tote bag. "Oh, and I'll need a
couple of large canvases and a sketch pad. You can pick
those up at the art store on your way to the hospital."

"Good Lord," Lee said. "How long are you staying?
The doctor told me it would be three days maximum.
The way you're gathering things up, you'll have enough
to keep you busy until the baby is eighteen. You *are*
planning to come back, aren't you?" He seemed worried.

When I felt the first twinge and the sudden urge to
bend over double and grasp my knees, I announced that
it was probably time to go to the hospital. By now the
suitcase was heavier than I was. Lee huffed and puffed
under his load of luggage as I sailed through the front
door of the medical center to give birth. If you didn't
count the doctor's cold fingers, my experience in the delivery room was uneventful though not something I'd
care to do every day. When they handed me a small,
perfect daughter, I knew I'd performed a miracle—
it had been worth all the throwing up early in the
morning.

Following Karen's birth I had so much to do I hardly
had time to look at her. She was tiny and precious. As I
fed her I read, wrote letters, and looked up names in the
telephone book. My roommate complained that just
watching so much activity made her stitches hurt; my
doctor complained that when he reached over to check
my pulse he dipped his hands in turpentine, and the
nurses complained because someone had been dash-
ing all over the hospital stealing newspapers. I had a
glorious time and hated to leave when my three days
were up.

By the time Claudia was born, I tucked a cheap comb
in my billfold and considered myself prepared.

"Where's your suitcase?" Lee asked when I told him we might as well call Grandma to stay with the other children, and then go on up to the hospital. "Aren't you taking anything with you?"

"Nope, not a thing."

"Not even baby announcements?"

"I'm not sending any. I'm beginning to hear rumors that when people see our return address on a little pink or blue envelope they chuck it in the garbage. I'm not giving them the opportunity to turn up their noses and say 'God, not again!'"

"Don't you even want lipstick?"

"No!"

"You'll scare the baby," he said.

"Might as well get it off to an honest start. What it sees now is what it's going to see later. I don't think it's fair to get the poor little thing's hopes up."

"How about a book?"

"I'm not going to read. I'm going to sleep."

"Candy for the nurses?"

"Let them buy their own candy. If you think I'm going to feed people who get joy out of an enema, you're wrong."

"I'll buy you a pretty nightgown," Lee said softly, touching my hair. "It's nearly spring. Wouldn't you like something bright and gay to welcome the spring and our new baby?" I paused for a minute, knowing he was right. It's being number seven didn't mean it was any less sensational. After all, spring had been around for thousands of years, and each time it came, its message of loveliness and hope was like a brand-new start . . . a brand-new feeling . . a brand-new expectation of faith and reassurance.

Could a baby be any less?

2

The Ruthless Booey-Bear Strikes Again

WHEN KAREN WAS A BABY, I read every book concerning child care that I could get my hands on. If it included pictures along with the text, I studied them carefully to see if I might possibly be missing something important. As I peered into the faces of quaint-looking mothers, I hoped desperately I'd find one who looked and felt as dumb as I did. Not a chance. Those mommies had everything under control. With peppy smiles they cradled contented babies in perfectly manicured hands while they looked seductively at handsome daddies through eyelashes eighteen inches long. My nails had been pared down to the cuticle following the first gouging of Karen's exposed pink bottom, and I hadn't had the energy to seduce anyone for weeks. In fact, I'd barely smiled. Well, maybe a flutter or two during those magic moments when Lee looked down at the two of us and said he was the luckiest guy in the world, but even on my good days my eyes looked a bit feverish.

You see, I'd swallowed that falsehood that happy babies don't cry. Nor do happy mothers. I thought I was happy. I thought our baby was happy too, but why then were both of us spending 80 percent of our waking hours in tears? "Nervous mothers make nervous babies," my mama scolded as she held Karen loosely in one arm

while she baked a pie with the other. The baby was so
relaxed she looked wilted.

"I've never been nervous in my life!" I twitched as a
cat meowed three blocks away.

"If all else fails, try a pacifier," she said, casually
propping Karen over one shoulder as she expertly mea-
sured, hemmed, and hung three pairs of curtains. A pacifier! Mama might as well have suggested arsenic. I
would not hear of such a thing. Lee, who had decided
long ago that two and a half hours of sleep per night
wasn't enough for a good day's work, agreed with her.
"Why not a pacifier?" he said. "Grandma wouldn't steer
us wrong." He went to the drugstore and bought six. I
promptly threw them in the garbage and declared that
if I needed such a crutch I must be a poor mother indeed. I continued to worry the daylights out of Karen by
snatching her from her bed each time she crooked an
elbow. When she crawled, I crawled beside her looking
for stray pins, lost pennies, and dropped thimbles. "She
could choke," I told Lee when he asked what I was doing
down on my hands and knees with my nose pressed into
the carpet. He brought home a playpen and I put the
magazine rack, two table lamps, all our ashtrays, and
the Christmas tree inside its bars and continued to
move about the house on all fours like a large, tearful
mother hippo. Karen was still crying and so was I, but
at least now we were doing it in a lot of different rooms.

My sister suggested I give her a favorite blanket to
sleep with. "It will give her a sense of security," she
said. Audrey had raised five sturdy boys who could fall
asleep on a ferris wheel; she couldn't get over my habit
of washing everything Karen owned at least fourteen
times a day. Most of Karen's blankets were either
trussed up in an automatic washer or lay huddled in the
laundry basket with three tiny spots of curdled milk on
them. "You're taking this clean business much too se-

riously," Audrey clucked. "A few germs won't hurt her." Thinking to myself that little girls were different (they aren't), I continued to dress Karen in nothing but white and washed her until her soft skin stretched like a shiny balloon. She was finding it harder and harder to cry because her tiny mouth was spread tight from so much soap and water.

"How about a drop or two of whiskey?" a sotty friend advised when Karen screamed through taut lips with teething pain. "Best home remedy in the world. People have used it for generations. Rub some on her gums and she'll pop off to sleep in no time." Or pop off to the detox ward at age two, I mumbled, and tossed that idea into the garbage can along with the pacifiers. I was determined to master motherhood without uncorking any spirits.

Six children later, I too could cook and caress at the same time, and I no longer had any misgivings about furnishing pacifiers to anyone who wanted them. We bought them by the gross and I distributed them among the children like pencils. We also had community gum as well as security blankets, security pillows, security dolls, and even security socks scattered all over the house. They were seldom washed and the fact that Augie-Doggie eventually shared each and every one of these things didn't bother me a bit. "A good dog lick never hurt anyone," was my motto. But to set the record straight, I never did resort to trickling straight shots down my children's throats or rubbing bourbon on their gums, though I can personally attest that a bit of Jack Daniel's with a twist of pablum doesn't taste so bad to me; and I haven't had a good cry in a long, long time.

Claudia was raised much more casually. About ten minutes following her birth, she discovered she had a passel of slaves at her command. The two majors were called Mom and Dad . . . lesser chattel brothers, sisters,

Grandma, Grandpa, uncles and aunts . . . cousins didn't count. A gentle dictator, she came straight home from the hospital and rearranged my complete social life. No longer were my best friends named Helen or Gwen or Betty Sue. I had a whole new bevy of bosom buddies called Booey-Bear, Bowwow, Quack Quack, and Pink Mousie. This quartet were constant companions during her growing-up years.

Pink Mousie gave me few problems. I simply put him in the bottom of the toy box, covered him with a few rubber blocks, and told Claudia that mice preferred dark places and that Mommy preferred not having a mousie pop up under her feet to scare her out of her wits. Quack Quack sat in the bathtub where ducks belong and Bowwow guarded the potty chair like a good dog. The ruthless Booey-Bear, however, controlled my entire life. Stuffed with fluff, red ribbon around his neck, he wore an innocent look in his glass eyes. He was soft, cuddly, and a real rip. That faky bear crawled into Claudia's crib and remained there just long enough to take over her affections, and then he disappeared.

"I can't sleep without Booey," she screamed. It was bedtime, and we couldn't find the bear.

"Booey is in the woods hunting for honey," I lied. "He'll be back tomorrow." I hoped.

"I won't sleep without Booey," she screamed, crawling over the rails of her crib.

"Booey-Bear will come home," I soothed, putting fat little legs back inside her bed. "He's gone on a teddy bears' picnic."

"I want Booey!" She was up and down in her crib like popcorn.

"Daddy will find Booey," I promised.

"Daddy doesn't know where Booey is," Lee admitted thirty minutes later. "Daddy has looked in the clothes hamper, the dresser drawers, the light fixtures, and the furnace. Old Booey-Bear has split," and he prepared to go to bed.

"Please find Booey," I begged. "I still have twenty dozen cookies to bake for Mary to take to school for the teacher's birthday. I can't spend all night hunting for a toy bear." Lee put on his robe, raised a fist in the air, and said something quite bad about bears.

"Daddy called Booey a naughty name," Claudia said in a shocked baby voice. "Daddy hates Booey." And she began to cry harder.

"Sssshhh, sweetheart, you'll wake up the other children. Daddy loves Booey. Mommy loves Booey. Daddy is tired. Mommy is tired," I sighed.

"*I want Booey!*" And over the crib railing she flew once again.

"Lord, we have got to find that bear," Lee said.

"Is he in the bathtub with Quack Quack?" I asked, hoping he was, and hoping Quack Quack had enough duck sense to sit on his head and hold him down beyond the count of three. Lee said he'd looked in the bathtub five times at least. "Maybe he's beneath the blocks with Pink Mousie," I hoped, and Lee said something about if he was we'd probably have a lot of little pinkish-brown, furry baby bears with big ears, whiskers, and long skinny tails. "I wouldn't put anything past that damned bear," he muttered going through the toy box for the tenth time. He didn't find Booey but he found his good belt.

"Did you look in the oven?" I softly questioned.

"Why would a toy bear be in the oven?"

"Because I put him there this morning," I sheepishly remembered. With one hand on the doorknob to facilitate a quick getaway, I explained that Bowwow had let down his guard for a split second, Booey had plunged into the potty chair, and I'd stuck him over the pilot light to dry and forgot him. Preheating the oven for

Mary's cookies had suddenly caused a smell of scorched bear fur to waft through our house and reminded me immediately where Booey might be. I dragged him, smoking from the oven. "Serves you right, Booey-fool," I whispered, wiping soot from his glass eyes before I put him on Claudia's pillow.

"He's nice and warm, Mommy." Claudia cuddled the burned bear close to her cheek and in three minutes she was sound asleep. Lee and I tiptoed from the room and went directly to the cupboard that held the Jack Daniel's. I've always said a good sip of whiskey after a bear hunt doesn't hurt anyone.

3

I'd Rather Be a Mother
Than a German
Shepherd

IT WASN'T LONG AFTER the day Booey-Bear nearly went to his death in the oven that I picked up the newspaper and read the real-estate ad that said "Split-level living at its best. Three bedrooms up, two down; living room, dining room, and kitchen; recreation room and laundry space in spacious lower level; all-purpose room attached to garage. Nice family home with charm." I wanted that house. We bought it and I waited for the charm to settle in. I dreamed of crisp, textured wallpapers, warm-colored ceramic tile, mirrors, coffee tables without gouges, and bathrooms. Oh, how I daydreamed of bathrooms. "Someday," I said to anyone who would listen, "I *will* have a house with five bathrooms." In the meantime, I stocked the one we did have with fourteen rolls of toilet tissue, nine bath towels, nine washcloths, lots of cheap, strong soap, shampoo, toothbrushes, razor blades, and Claudia's potty chair; and Quack Quack was joined by a plastic bucket of other playthings.

There was no room to walk around, and if Amy or Claudia joined me, which they usually did, I had to back in and out of the room and sit sideways. Lee yelled that he'd been bayoneted in the butt by a floating platoon of toy soldiers so often while bathing that he was beginning to walk funny. I woke up in the middle of the night

28

to the wail of a sleepy Claudia. Gathering child, security blanket, and Booey-Bear, and stumbling and yawning down the hallway, I entered the bitsy bathroom. I knew my way so well I didn't bother to turn on lights; it wasn't unusual for me to bring both bare feet down firmly on eight jacks, twelve marbles, and three bayonets—all placed carefully in front of the door. My scream of "Dear God, I've broken my foot!" not only brought Lee up from a sound sleep but terrorized Claudia, causing her to drop blanket and Booey into the dark crevices behind the bathroom stool. Poor Baby. Poor Blanket. Poor Booey. Poor Mommy.

This small bathroom became a convention center early in the morning before work, school, and breakfast. I could stand outside its door and hear the whole panorama of a happy American family unfold.

"Make him move, Mother. He's standing in front of the mirror." Karen had John firmly by the ear.

"You told me I had to wash at least once this week, Mom, remember?" John called out in agony. "You told me that last night at the supper table. Well, I'm trying, but she won't let me."

"Where's Booey? I can't find Booey. I can't go poo-poo without Booey!"

"She took my shoes. I can't go to school without shoes."

"There's hair in the sink. AAAAAAaaaaaaaaagh!!!"

"Make her stop taking the toilet paper, Mom. She stuffs it in her sweater. I've seen her do it."

"My toothbrush is wet. If he used my toothbrush on Augie again I'm going to throw up!"

"I am going to throw up if you all don't get out of here right this minute and go to your rooms." This immediately cleared the bathroom of children, dog, and mother. Even Booey sprang up from behind the stool

and got the hell out. Lee wanted the bathroom all to himself and he knew just how to get it.

For this small bathroom we had an enormous hot-water heater. In fact, it was the largest one manufactured in our area, outside of those used in metropolitan hospitals and laundromats. When it was installed, the plumber sat back on his haunches, wiped the sweat from his brow, and warned me that if it ever exploded we'd take half the town with us. This brought such horrible scenes to my mind that I wouldn't let Lee turn it up past lukewarm. We never had any hot water.

"Why did I spend two thousand dollars for sixty-two thousand five hundred BTR's and I still have to shave in ice?" he whined.

"Because," I told him, "if I turn it up high I can hear it spit. I'm afraid it will explode."

"It won't explode. It has a pressure valve."

"Someone stuffed gum in that. When I dug it out, the doo-hickey got stuck. I don't think it works anymore."

"Did you call the plumber?"

"He wouldn't come. Said it was too damn dangerous." His attitude didn't surprise me. During our one-bathroom days, I suppose a hundred or more sad plumbers marched in and out of our house. One by one they came, optimistic with their years of training and experience, only to leave defeated by apple cores, rubber dog bones, and Booey-Bear eyes. I could almost hear the wheels click as each one I called tried his best to invent a way to get out of making a house call.

"Gosh, I'd like to help you out, lady," Mr. Plumber said. "But my truck is broken."

"I'll come and get you," I volunteered.

"I hurt my arm."

"I have some nice ointment that will fix you right up."

"I've lost my tools."

"You can borrow mine." I didn't have any, but he didn't know that.

"I'm tired."

"I'm tired, too," I cried out. "Tired of hauling my children to the neighbors' every time they have to go to the bathroom. The neighbors are locking their screen doors and pretending they don't hear me knock."

"I'm sorry," he said, but I could tell I was beginning to get to him.

"Furthermore," I continued, "my husband said if he had to come home one more day to a house without a bathroom we'd have to move to a motel, and with seven children we certainly can't afford that." The plumber obviously wasn't a hardhearted man. He was a professional and enjoyed fooling around with pipes, augers, and vises. He took pride in his work. He just didn't like working at our house, and I guess I couldn't blame him. David crouched beside him as he worked, offering advice and a sticky lick from a sucker while Augie-Doggie patiently snuffled about his feet waiting for a bone to emerge from the depths of the sewer.

"Can the little boy and the dog go outside to play?" he suggested as he dropped to his knees to look into our bathroom stool. "God, there's a lot of junk in here. Don't you people have any wastebaskets?"

"Of course we have wastebaskets. One in every room."

"Well, you could save a lot of money and wear and tear on your plumbing if you could get the children to use them instead of tossing everything in the pot." Removing David's foot from the middle of his back, he picked up a fingerful of crumbling tile that hovered around the faucet. "I'd make them quit splashing so much. They're ruining your walls."

"The little ones like to play in the water," I said.

"Take them to the beach."

"In the middle of March?"

"What does your husband think of this?" His eyes swept about the rather dismal little room. I didn't think

that was any of his business, but I couldn't afford to irri-
tate him with the job only half finished. Gritting my
teeth, I told him I could usually soothe things over if
defective flushers, puny pulldowns, and beat-up ball
flappers were mentioned when the bill was itemized. "Is
there any reason why you have to say anything about
finding dishcloths, doll clothes, and dominoes in there
when you send the bill? Don't say anything, please," I
begged. "Let's not clutter my husband's head with
trivia. He has enough to worry about with high taxes
and low social-security benefits." This was an excellent
move on my part, for now I'd diverted his attention from
our plumbing to national affairs. He enthusiastically
launched into a lengthy discussion of inflation, the state
of the union, and how our government was going to hell
in a handbasket. I stood in the doorway, clucking my
tongue wisely.

"Did you know," he shouted, waving a plumber's
snake in my face, "that the Big Board totaled forty-one-
point-one shares?"

"That's a rotten shame," I cried out, pressing both
arms to my bosom and looking shocked. "What's the
world coming to!" I had no idea what he was talking
about. The only Big Board I was familiar with was Monopoly.

"And composite indexes are dropping!" he continued,
his eyes nearly popping out of his head with excitement.

"Sonofagun!" I exclaimed, pretending vertigo at such
a possibility.

"It's a damn sad day when a poor working stiff can't
make a go out of the stock market," and he sat there in
a daze. Out of the corner of my eye I watched as David,
bored with the turn of events, picked up an expensive
ratchet set and headed toward his bedroom. Excusing
myself, I chased David down, catching him just as he
was about to remove his closet doors from their hinges. I

raced back upstairs and found Mr. Plumber, shaken and pale, pinned in the bathtub with Augie, fur raised and gums slicked back to show every tooth in his head, standing above him. I shoved a growling Augie out of the bathroom, told him to go to bed with David, and assured the plumber no one would hurt him.

"My cousin's a plumber," he shouted as he rose from the tub, gathered his tools, and ran toward the front door. "Next time call him!" I found out later the two of them hadn't spoken to each other for fourteen years.

I posted a sign in the bathroom that read "DO NOT THROW THINGS IN THE STOOL!" This worked fine with Lee—he wasn't prone to tossing anything in there anyway—and Karen, Susan, John, David, and Mary promised "on their honor" they would be very careful, especially with such a large sign . . . and larger mother . . . reminding them. But Amy, Claudia, and Augie couldn't read so they kept right on messing up the plumbing. I decided everything was much nicer in my dreams. It had become a habit of mine to set aside a few minutes each morning before I climbed out of bed to think about how it could be, how it *must* be, in homes, like my neighbor Helen's, where things were organized and efficient. I imagined my bedroom slippers, both of them, standing straight and fluffy, toes pointed toward the east, at the foot of our bed, just where I'd left them the night before. In my dreams I didn't find one crumpled under the rocking chair and the other, its furry sole mashed by a dog tongue, near the back door.

Drifting deliciously on a dream cloud, I saw myself in a lovely, thin peignoir slipping into our bathroom where I found each bath towel hung straight on proper rods. Not one was tossed on the floor, damp and fringed with dirt, rendering it unfit for human use. Everything was bright and sparkly clean. Nothing ran over when I flushed. Even Quack Quack was polished.

"Good morning," a cheerful voice said.

"A stranger is in our house," I shuddered. "I will be attacked, molested, and maybe killed." And so early in the morning too. Oh, well, at least I'd go with matching bedroom slippers, and the bathroom would look nice for condolence calls. I swung around, expecting to see a smiling maniac. It was only Lee, and he *never* smiles before he has his morning coffee. Sometimes he doesn't smile before dinner either. In fact, quite often he doesn't smile all day; but there he was standing in the doorway looking very happy. Wow! It was some dream.

Someone had plugged in the coffee, ham and eggs were sizzling on the stove, and the orange juice was so fresh it was almost dishonorable. On an ordinary, non-dreamlike day it has a slight tuna-fish flavor.

"No bologna sandwiches for breakfast today," I marveled. I hoped I'd never awake from this dream. But the children were up. I could hear footsteps in the hallway. Dreams are nice while they last, I decided, but here come the kids . . . the day will get off to its usual barbaric start. I was totally wrong. Each child had combed hair and was dressed in the exact clothing that I'd laid out. Karen and John were holding hands. This was almost more than I could handle, dream or no dream. As they sat at the table, napkins folded primly in their laps, I looked at their little wooden faces, poised to be sure, but with no personalities, and the thought entered my mind that I really wouldn't want such a bunch of puny children, even in a dream.

Going into the living room, I noticed that not one of my houseplants had died during the night. The African violet even had two purple flowers. It was eight years old and had never produced a bloom in its life. "You are beautiful, African violet," I crooned, and one more flower opened right before my astonished eyes. "Imagine, you haven't been watered in three weeks and still you bloom." Take that, prissy Helen, I said to myself. Helen raised African violets with stems like oak trees and flowers so vivid they hurt your eyes.

Eventually, of course, I had to climb out of bed and wake up to the fact that I didn't live in a dream world but the *real* world and that my houseplants did die without warning, our bathroom was messy, and the children, whose clothing had turned from riches to rags, were starving for breakfast and very, very cross. Lee had cut himself shaving and had tiny pieces of toilet paper plastered to his chin, and my exotic peignoir had turned to flannel. From that moment on, it was back to normal; and when Susan said she had to write a two-page essay before she went to school, I fussed at her because she'd waited until the last minute to do her homework.

"It's about you, Mom," she said. "I have to compare my mother to a well-known personality. It can be fact or fiction."

"That should be easy," I said, throwing my shoulders back and tilting my head in a regal manner. "There's Queen Elizabeth to draw from."

"Be serious," Susan giggled.

"I *am* serious."

"How about the German shepherd down the street," John suggested. He was, at the moment, recovering from a series of motherly growls after being caught with his hand in the cookie jar before he'd finished eating his cereal. I gave him a dirty look and ignored him as much as I could.

"You could use the rabbit for comparison," Karen howled, looking around the table to see if her wit had been properly appreciated.

"Mommy doesn't have long ears," Amy said. "Why are you big kids laughing? Daddy doesn't think it's funny."

I shook my finger and told everyone to keep their mouths shut.

"I've got it," David shouted. "Mount St. Helen's"— and he squinted his eyes in my direction, sizing me up, no doubt, for lava flow. "We never know when you're going to erupt." For a minute there I'd thought his idea was quite good. Mountains are stately, magnificent, and often gorgeous. I wouldn't mind being compared to a mountain.

"How about Scrooge?" someone suggested.

"That's Daddy," another said. Lee had left the room to go peel the paper from his face—they could say that in comfort and safety. Mary, clapping her hands, shouted, "I know just the one! Mommy's like the Old Woman in the Shoe! She has so many children she doesn't know what to do," and in a singsong voice Mary recited the nursery rhyme twice and was starting on "Little Jack Horner" when I patted her curly head, told her she was pretty close to the truth, but that Mommy had Daddy to help her and the poor woman who lived in a shoe was all alone. I didn't add, however, that you'd never catch me with my shoelaces down like that poor thing. Not once in that entire nursery rhyme does anyone mention who is paternally responsible for all of those children. A chorus of ideas tumbled forth as Susan tried desperately to write down the suggestions as fast as they called them out.

"Arnold Palmer!" Everyone laughed. My golf game is lousy and they knew it.

"Betty Crocker!" More laughter.

"Dolly Parton!" Everyone looked stunned except Lee, who had returned to the room, still wounded but with no paper hanging from his nose, and he looked wistful. "I have just the one," he said. I held my breath. I wasn't sure I wanted to hear. "Your mom is a lot like Mother Earth." I didn't know if I should be complimented or hit him, but the more I thought about it the more I decided he was probably right. I suppose I was a little bit like Mother Earth. I'm round just like she is and I'm soft in some places and quite crusty in others. I, too, blossom in the springtime and curl up my toes when it gets cold. I'm dusty around the edges and, Lord knows, there's no denying I've proven myself fertile and productive. Mother Earth and I had an awful lot in common if you wanted to sit down and compare notes.

I'm sure she gets as tired as I do. Just look at all of the people she has to go around picking up after, not to mention the dogs, cats, birds, squirrels, and other animals that mess up her floors. "I bet that's why we have earthquakes," I said. "Mother Earth must get mad just like I do when I have to go around cleaning up after all of you." John said he didn't think Susan's teacher would buy that theory.

"Oh, she might," I told him. "Especially if I invite her over to see your room and then tell her to hang around and listen to what happens if you don't pick it up before your grandmother visits. Then she'll see how I can make the windows rattle and the floor shake, and it won't be Mother Earth that makes it happen but Mother Lueth. I think I could convince her." And obviously Mother Earth felt the same way about sunsets and small babies as I did because we had so many of them. "Yes," I told Susan, "use Mother Earth. I like it. I'd be very proud of the comparison."

Besides, it's better than a German shepherd.

4

To the Country, the Country, to Buy a Fat Pig

TOWARD THE END of March, Lee bounced into the house with a triumphant smile on his face and a six-page, color brochure under his arm. "Guess what I just bought," he said.

Oh, God, I thought, I'm finally going to get a trash compactor.

"Daddy, Daddy," Mary dashed into her father's arms. "Am I getting a canopy bed?"

"It's a new hunting dog." John and David danced with glee, and Augie sat down hard and hung his head. Karen and Susan closed their eyes, clasped hands, and prayed for a red sports car.

"Is it bigger than a breadbasket?" I asked.

"It's nothing like that," Lee declared, spreading the brochure out on the dining-room table. A dozen enameled deep freezes, all with hind quarters of beef, baskets stuffed with homemade pies and cookies, bags of frozen vegetables, fruits, and breads stared back from the pages. Pointing at the one packed from top to toe with food, he said, "I bought this one. It will save us a lot of money and time. We'll all benefit from the vitamins, we'll have a huge garden, and we'll freeze every bean and pea we raise, not to mention carrots, squash, corn, and zucchini. We'll have enough food to see us through summer, fall, and winter. We might not even have to go to the grocery store again as long as we live."

The children groaned. Unless someone could quickly invent a way to freeze potato chips and Cheerios, their gourmet days were over.

"I don't know how to freeze food," I wailed.

"Ask Helen. She does it all the time." This was certainly true. At least once a week Helen called me over to admire her deep freeze. It was jammed with pecan rolls, shrimp gumbo, and cauliflower puffs. We stood, shivering from the blast of cold air rolling up from the coils of the freezer, and inventoried the food she had prepared that week.

"We'll never starve," she said happily. "And it gives Ray such a feeling of security and independence to know our larder is stocked with well-prepared frozen foods. Why, we could have a dozen people drop in unexpectedly and all I have to do is reach in my freezer and I can feed them like kings."

I became so paranoid about filling up that freezer that for the first few weeks it sat in the utility room, I could hardly think of anything else. I spent enough on plastic bags, boxes, and Ball jars to keep our family in groceries for six months. I read instruction sheets and recipe books and was bored to death. I longed to go back to a good, polished love story with a bit of sordid sex thrown in. There was very little romance in a broccoli leaf. I mulled over terms like *blanch, scald, ascorbic acids, bacteria, enzymes, freezer burn.* Scared to death someone would accidentally bump into the cord and dislodge the plug, I checked the freezer five or six times a day, fully expecting to see hundreds of dollars' worth of food swimming in defrosted water. For a while the responsibility of the freezer drove me crazy, and then the newness wore off and I turned my attentions to important things, like tying a tail on a kite for David, oiling

Claudia's tricycle for nice spring day travels, sweeping the sidewalks of winter debris, and enjoying the sounds of bird songs. Lee ruffled cold hands through a stack of cheap pizzas and sprinkled-down laundry and told me the freezer should hold food, not anchovies and his good shirts. He felt we weren't taking full advantage of an important and expensive appliance.

"What can we do?" I was a freezer failure, and Lee knew it. He'd been kind about it, but I could tell his patience was wearing thin.

"Perhaps we could buy some meat," he said. "We could save on pork, I know, if we bought half a hog at one time. Ray said he'd take the other half. He knows a farmer who would have it professionally wrapped, packaged, and labeled. All we have to do is drive out and pick it up." This sounded fine to me. Frankly, I could hardly wait to sink my teeth into some good homegrown pork chops. My grandfather butchered his own hogs and I remembered with spicy pleasure the good taste of fresh sausages and crackly chitlins that dripped grease down my chin. Of course, I'd closed my eyes when Grandpa hung the poor pigs up by little fat feet and rammed a sharp knife in their throats and split them open, and I was never allowed to inspect some of the more private ingredients that caused Grandpa, the hired man, and my dad to clap each other on the back and exclaim in masculine tones: "Now *that's* what I call a real hog!"

The children were elated that we were finally going to put something in our freezer to be proud of. They were growing tired of trying to explain to Helen's children why ours held no icy and secret surprises. "They think we're poor," John said. Surely now, with a full load, his status in the neighborhood would soar. He still thought a hunting dog would've been better but a dead hog was at least something to brag about.

We made a day of picking up our pig. Bundling everyone into sweaters and jeans, I packed sandwiches and lemonade, plunked Claudia in her car seat, rearranged the back of the station wagon so there would be enough room for our pig to travel comfortably, and led happy songs as we traveled down the road. "To the country, the country, to buy a fat pig," I jollied, encouraging everyone to join in. Karen thought she was much too old for such foolishness but I noticed that once in a while she jiggled her head in time to the music as the rest of us sang and clapped our hands.

The farmer and his wife were a gracious, warm couple. They welcomed us with cries of "Now you-all get out of the car and make yourselves to home. Let the children run around and see the little animals." And this was a fine idea until a big, honking goose took two or three pecks out of Claudia's denim bottom and David threatened to kill it with his bare hands. For a minute there, I thought I might have to learn how to freeze a quickly purchased dead goose, but the farmer's wife saved the moment (and her goose) by calling from her kitchen door that she had cold milk and lemon cookies for everybody. We ate while boxes and boxes of neatly sealed bundles of meat went into the station wagon as Lee helped the farmer load. I came outside to watch, munching on a lemon cookie that melted like snow the minute it hit my tongue, and the farmer, proudly looking at our packed wagon, said, "That's going to be nice for you, isn't it, missus? Having all that fine pork at your fingertips."

"It certainly is," I agreed. "Thank God, I'm going to know what to cook for the next few weeks, at least. No more guessing and scrambling around in a freezer full of crusts and collars." The farmer looked puzzled and turned to Lee for an explanation, but he'd bolted for the house to gather up the children. He had absolutely no intention of explaining to a man who obviously had a

wife domesticated enough to bake cookies in the afternoon that he was stuck with one that stocked a freezer
with clean clothes. We said pleasant good-byes, shook
hands all around, thanked them for their hospitality
and their pig, and as we started to leave the driveway,
the farmer leaned into the car, tenderly stroked one of
the boxes, and whispered, "Good-bye, Ace."

"Who's Ace?" I asked.

"The pig," he answered sadly.

"What pig?" Down deep I really didn't want to know.

"The one you're taking home for your freezer."

"Did you hear what he just said," I punched Lee.
"That poor pig has a name." A great hush came over the
backseat as the children huddled together as far from
the boxes of meat as they could get, and Mary burst into
great, sobbing tears. I turned to Lee with a tight white
face. "I can't cook that pig now that I've been introduced
to him. I can't eat him either." Lee clenched his teeth
and told me not to make a scene. "We'll talk about it
later," he hissed. "Besides, it's no different than the
bacon you buy in the store." Well, I knew better than
that. Stubbornly squaring my body, I told him I hadn't
bargained with biting into something that had obviously run about its pigsty, carefree and squealing, secure in the knowledge that it wasn't anonymous but
loved. People don't name things they don't like, I said.

In my heart I could see Ace's pink nose quivering
with devotion for his master, all innocence and affec-
tion; pure and proud of his name. He wasn't going to end
up in *my* frying pan. I gave the farmer a dirty look as
we drove out of the driveway toward home. He'd certainly fooled me, he and his cookie-baking wife. Here I'd
thought they were such a nice couple. They didn't seem
the type that would sell a family friend. "You can never
tell about people," I told Lee as we drove silently down
the road. I say silently, because the children were very,

very quiet. Usually they fought and bit as we traveled, but today they were as quiet as water. Perhaps, I thought, we should always carry a dead pig with us when we traveled.

Throughout that entire spring, Lee continued to think I was going to serve Ace for dinner. "Do I smell something good tonight?" he'd say, rubbing his hands together in anticipation. "I just bet we're having pork chops."

"Guess again!" I told him. "We're having goulash."

"Tomorrow night we're having pork chops?" he questioned hopefully.

"Tomorrow night we have left-over goulash." And so it went. He kept asking for pork chops and I kept serving goulash, but eventually I ran out of goulash. I was halfway through the cookbook borrowed from Helen on 1,001 ways to serve hamburger when Lee put his husbandly foot down and insisted I serve the pork. "And try to do it cheerfully," he said.

I served it all right, but I didn't do it cheerfully. Ace appeared in several dishes accompanied by a funeral like atmosphere. I felt like a pallbearer as I sadly carried a fried, baked, or boiled Ace to the table, his remains wreathed with bits of parsley to show my respects. Lee raised his eyes toward the heavens and commented that he expected to hear organ peals of "Whispering Hope" coming from the light fixtures as he ate. The two boys recovered fast from the shock of eating someone's favorite pet and, like their father, smacked their lips over huge helpings of poor Ace, causing the girls to gag and swear they'd never eat pork again for the rest of their lives. I longed for the day when I would no longer be forced to serve Ace and eggs for breakfast. Then Easter arrived, and with it Alexander, and I completely forgot all about mourning a pig.

*　　*　　*

Before I married and became a mother, my Easters at home had been one of new shoes, a pretty pink or lavender dress, Sunday school, and baskets of hard-boiled eggs dyed in rainbow colors. I loved looking at those eggs because I wasn't allowed to eat them. My mother told me they were poison. I have no idea *why* mama told me this but I took her word for it and was almost too scared to even handle them. I wondered many times during my childhood why the Easter bunny would bring poisoned eggs to little kids but I was young and *I* didn't question my mother.

On our first Easter together, I was astonished to see my new husband nonchalantly roll and crack the eggs we'd happily dyed so many pretty colors the night before, preparing to actually eat them for breakfast.

"Stop!" I cried out. "Don't eat those eggs! They're poison!" Was he so tired of me in the few short weeks we'd been married that he would take his life with an Easter egg right before my eyes? Lee patiently explained there was absolutely nothing wrong with those eggs. "I've been eating them for years," he said and to demonstrate how safe they really were he ate three, without salt, pepper, or mayonnaise. He didn't keel over, and I started to doubt some of my mother's theories—including the one she'd passed on about ducks.

Like most little children, I'd always yearned for a soft, fluffy yellow duckling to play with at Eastertime. A live one with real feathers, one that quacked and waddled. My mother told me they were dangerous and that they, too, were poison. "Ducks can be the most vicious animals in the world," she explained, shaking her apron fearfully, "and when they get angry they spit poison." This was pretty hard for me to swallow because they looked so cute and precious in the feed-store window, but I believed her; kids of the 1930s were pretty dumb. I went through most of my early life terrified of colored eggs and little ducks. Alexander split that old mother's tale right in two. He was a supreme duck. A king. A prince of drakes.

Tiny, adorable, and the color of fresh cream when we brought him home from the chicken shop, he lived in a pasteboard box on top of the washing machine. His favorite pastime was eating crackers and flipping crumbs into his water dish. He sat contentedly in a child's hand, watching *Captain Kangaroo, Sesame Street,* and *Police Woman,* enjoying nursery rhymes and nude violence as only a duck can. When he grew old enough to get in and out of the box on his own, he listened for the alarm in the early morning, jumped out of his box, and beat Lee to the bathroom. "Jesus," Lee said, "few men are greeted by a duck pulling on their pajama legs before they shave in the morning." But he liked Alexander as much as the rest of us did.

For some reason, Alexander didn't quack. Perhaps it was because he lived with people and none of us quacked. When he was angry, wanted to make a point, or was hungry, he simply tilted his head to one side and opened his mouth. A slight hissing sound came from the holes in his beak but no quacks. I looked "duck" up in the encyclopedia, to see if he was possibly suffering from some sort of disease, and discovered information about mating habits, nesting, and how ducks flew, but nothing about quacks. I reassured the children by telling them Alexander was polite like their father, and that since he had nothing important to say he chose to remain silent. "When he feels the time has come, he'll open up," I promised.

When Mary gave him a soapy bath, washing all of the natural grease from his feathers, nearly drowning him, and waterlogging him for thirty minutes, Alexander almost quacked. But he didn't. Instead he patiently lay, very clean, until his feathers dried and the normal oils returned. Probably he would've liked to quack. He just hadn't figured out how to.

As Alexander grew to full manhood, or whatever it is ducks grow to, Lee began to feel sorry for him. Although there were plenty of children, cats, dogs, and squirrels in the neighborhood, there were no other ducks. Alexander was still following Lee into the bathroom in the morning but he was doing strange things. "He's pecking hell out of the toilet paper," Lee explained, showing me a roll with teeny dots and beak holes breaking through to the cardboard tubes.

"He's never done that before," I said. "I wonder why he's so nervous."

Lee raised one eyebrow and pointed out—again— that Alexander was the only duck on the block. "There aren't even any girl ducks," he said, "if you get my meaning."

"I don't think that's the reason," I shook my head. "It's like quacking. If he doesn't know about it, how can he miss it?"

Lee told me to go to the encyclopedia and look up "instinct"; and he gathered the children, Alexander, and a sack of milo seed and, loading everyone in the car, drove to the pond in a park eight blocks from our house. He said later that he really and truly thought turning Alexander loose in a more natural habitat would relax some of his nervous tensions. The park pond was dotted with domestic and wild ducks throughout the year and looked like a perfect spot for Le Duck to rid himself of male frustrations. If indeed he had any. Lee thought if he left Alexander there for a day or two and then brought him back home, he'd be in a better disposition and would leave our toilet paper alone. Unfortunately, Alexander was nearly murdered by his own kind.

An excited group of children, bearing a duck with an amazed look on his face, returned from the pond trip and in unison told me that Daddy had tried to kill Alexander.

"Well, it wasn't actually Dad," Karen admitted. "It was the other ducks. The minute Dad set Alex in the water the others attacked him and tried to beat him to death with their wings. We tried throwing milo seeds at them, but it didn't help. They flapped and flapped and Daddy finally waded out and got him."

"Did Alexander quack?" I asked.

"No, but Daddy said some bad words," Amy observed.

As Alexander grew older he didn't seem to mind being deprived of duck sex. He spent his days in beautiful duck abandon, stalking Augie, preening his feathers in mud puddles, walking about in the gutter, and ripping cookies right out of Claudia's hands. His nights were spent dreaming duck dreams in his box in the utility room. He wasn't housebroken but I tried to forgive him.

When Alexander finally learned to quack, it was triggered by a powerful fright. Left to his own duck devices one Sunday afternoon while we took a family outing at a local department store, Alexander walked into Ray's garden and pulled out the young, tender shoots in the pea patch. Ray didn't want to murder Alexander in cold blood but thought he definitely should be taught a valuable lesson. So, grabbing the duck in one arm, a ladder in the other—according to Helen, who watched from across the street—Ray marched into our yard, placed the ladder against the side of the house, and climbed, dragging a surprised duck behind him. Alexander was left standing on the roof of our house. And there we found him, backed up against the chimney, and quacking for the whole world to hear. Once he learned, he didn't stop until he died. It was a vibrant sound—one that Augie, in particular, despised, and one that the rest of us eventually grew used to. Lee said, however, he almost wished the duck had never learned how and had stuck to eating toilet paper.

Personally, I loved hearing it. And I loved old Alexander. He was a happy family memory.

5

A Diary Is a Very Personal Thing

"A DIARY IS a very personal thing," I lectured John and David. I had them sitting on the couch in the living room, feet on the floor, hands in their laps. As the April morning sun chipped its way through our waxy window, I explained that they should know better than to search their sisters' rooms for the private, innermost thoughts that go into a young girl's diary.

"We didn't have to search, Mom," John said. "Susan's was on the floor by her bed and Karen had hers on the dresser. All we had to do was pick 'em up."

"Did you read them?" I asked, exploring their faces carefully to see if they were telling the truth. Sometimes they fooled me and did. Karen had screeched madly for an hour and said she'd never be able to face her friends again if they told anybody what was in her diary, and Susan threatened to punch both of them in the nose.

"I read Susan's," David admitted. "It was pretty boring and there were a lot of jelly smears on the pages. There wasn't anything in there worth getting punched in the nose for." John agreed that Karen's wasn't too great either. "All she talked about," he said, "was seeing Joe Somebody in the hallway and saying hi to him, and then she wrote about what he was wearing. She even

49

described his socks, Mom, and she can't spell. She only
put one *s* in passion." I swallowed hard and stifled the
urge to run quickly to Karen to ask her what exactly did
she know about passion. I also wondered how John, at
twelve, was so sure of the spelling.

"You can read *my* diary." Mary had wandered into
the room with a wide-lined cheap tablet in her hand.
She proudly held it up for all of us to admire. John
sneered that anyone who still printed her name in block
letters sure couldn't have much good stuff in a diary,
and Mary burst into insulted tears. Soothing her, I
promised her that I'd love to read what she'd printed as
soon as I prescribed a suitable punishment for her two
brothers. Snooping was a middle-of-the-road crime,
somewhere between not coming home after school and
jumping up and down on the bed. I took away their basketball, put it on the mantel, and told them it had to
stay there for a week; then maybe next time they'd
learn to keep their hands off things that didn't belong to
them. I wasn't fond of having a basketball as the focal
point of my mantel decor, but we weren't planning on
having any company so I supposed it wouldn't matter;
this way I could keep an eye on it and be sure they
didn't sneak it out behind my back.

Their interest in reading diaries bothered me more
than having a basketball in our living room, because I
happened to know that somewhere in our basement,
tucked away in a large barrel, were my keepsakes from
high school, college, and my premarital flings. I·hadn't
been "flung" much, but, scattered together with the
scrapbooks, report cards, letters, my sorority pin, pictures of classmates were three imitation leather-bound
volumes of my past, all written in great detail and with
a helluva lot of imagination. I'd started keeping a diary
when I was eleven years old and ran the volumes
through until my junior year in high school, when I be-

came too busy living my life to write about it. Until then, 90 percent of what was written I had made up, borrowing a major portion from the books I sneaked under my pillow and from a friend who had started kissing boys in the sixth grade. They weren't exactly lies . . . only a young girl taking a literary license. Yet someone who lived in the exact, precise, and literal way of my husband would never, never understand that I really hadn't planned to run off with my math teacher for cocktails at the age of thirteen.

In reality the math teacher was middle-aged, balding, very married, very harried, and hated us all so much he wouldn't speak to us in the halls let alone go out for cocktails. But Lee would never believe that. He would see him as a lecherous slicker who had only taken up teaching so he could prey on innocent girls. I'd never be able to convince him, if he read my diary, that I'd hoked up the math teacher in order to make my daily entries more exciting than fractions. It was an adolescent's way of passing the time pleasantly when there was nothing better to do than dry dishes. We didn't have television. All I had were my fantasies, and I didn't want to share them with my family. Especially my husband.

"What should I do?" I asked Helen, who'd come over to borrow some navy-blue thread and now stood in the middle of the room, staring at the basketball that sat between two pewter candlesticks, a delicate porcelain vase, and our wedding picture.

"If you like, I could take your diaries home with me," she offered.

"Not on your life," I told her.

"I wouldn't read them, if that's what you're insinuating."

"Oh, yes, you would. You know you would." I thanked her for her interest and said I'd take care of it myself. She went away miffed but I knew she'd be back. Our house was so much more interesting than hers.

That very next morning, I made a decision. I'd hardly slept the night before because I could swear I heard someone poking around in our basement going through my souvenir barrel. It was time I threw those diaries away. After all, wasn't I married? I had my true love; the days of dreaming of a prince charming were behind me. Maybe my present prince drove a clunky station wagon instead of a white steed, and moonlit nights were, more than likely, spent going over utility bills, but he was *there,* wasn't he? And I certainly wanted him to stay and I'd feel much more secure about that if those diaries were gone. Putting Claudia down for a nap with Booey-Bear, I pawed through the barrel, picked up the three diaries, and, without even giving them a last reading, I marched straight from the basement to the backyard garbage can, tossed them in, dusted off my hands, and forgot about them . . . until I looked out the kitchen window one hour later and saw the garbage truck parked in our alley with its motor turned off.

I couldn't imagine why the gentleman in the gray coveralls was sitting there in our alley, in his truck, with the motor off, bent over the steering wheel, with a tiny brown imitation leather-bound book in his hands while his shoulders heaved, and his face was lit up like a sunburst—that man was reading my diary! He was reading every word. I could tell because between pages he'd glance up at our house with a hint of pure lust on his face. Until that moment I'd enjoyed the reputation of being a nice lady, durable and semi-dull, but if this garbage man went through our neighborhood repeating what he'd just read, we'd have to move. It was as simple as that. I couldn't just stand there watching him lick his lips. I had to do something.

He was so absorbed in my sordidness that he didn't realize I was sneaking up to the side of the truck. Actually, I was flying up to the side of the truck. My feet hardly touched the ground. *"Give me that book!"* I screamed through his open window and, tearing the diary from his hands, I clawed across his lap for the other two volumes he'd laid aside for bedtime reading. I raced back into the house, leaving the stunned garbage man to nurse a welt across the back of his hand where my fingernail had removed a quarter of an inch of flesh. He sat there for a full ten minutes before he slowly and deliberately banged his way down the alley and out of sight.

Naturally, it would've made a better story if the two of us had stood around and chatted about the contents of my diary for an hour or two, but I had absolutely no intention of ever seeing that man again, let alone holding a conversation with him. I hadn't looked at his face ... just his lap ... and I prayed with all my heart he hadn't looked at my face. I hated to think that every time he picked up our empty soup cans and limp lettuce leaves he was going to recall the steamy pages of my diary.

Lee thought the entire incident served me right and turned down my request for a built-in incinerator so we could burn our own garbage. That night I tore up the diaries, page by page, struck a match, and watched as the smoke curled toward the heavens, bearing my fictitious wantonness upward, no doubt amusing the angels sitting on the clouds while the children roasted wienies on long sticks over my bonfire. From that day on, I simply drew the drapes when I knew it was time for the trash to be picked up, and hid behind the couch.

"If you'd throw things away when they've outlived their usefulness, this wouldn't happen," Lee said. "You should've gotten rid of those damn diaries years ago." I could hardly believe my ears. This was coming from a man who still had the first bent nail of his childhood! But tossing the diaries had motivated me into thinking about doing some spring housecleaning. Lord only knew, it needed it. With the few warm April days we'd been having, we'd devoted nearly every free minute and every ounce of labor to cleaning up outside. The lawn and garden didn't look too bad. It was inside the house that the weeds were growing.

Little spiders merrily made their webs comfortable with no interruption as they set up vacation houses in the corner of the dining room. A newspaper had taken root under the coffee table, gum wrappers bloomed behind the couch, the sweet scent of ripe tube socks permeated the air, and dust nodules dipped and swayed in the twilight. Our carpet was freshly sodded with junk and, oh, how I wished someone would invent a riding vacuum cleaner.

"First things first!" I said. Drawing up a large sign, I posted it on the refrigerator door, where I knew everyone would look when they came home from school.

IT IS SPRING AND THIS HOUSE IS A MESS AND I INTEND TO CLEAN IT UP AND I INTEND TO HAVE HELP CLEANING IT. WE CANNOT AFFORD A HOUSEKEEPER. YOUR FATHER SAYS SO. THEREFORE, IT IS UP TO EVERYONE WHO LIVES HERE TO DO THEIR PART.

And I signed it

YOUR MOTHER!!

"What's it say, Mommy?" Claudia asked, peering up

at the big note on the refrigerator door. "There aren't any pictures."

I picked her up, gave her a hug, told her it said that Mommy was very, very tired, was probably going to have a bad headache, and wouldn't it be nice if she'd pull all of her toys out from under her bed and put them nicely in the toy box where they belonged.

"I can do that," she said proudly and ran to her room, disappearing under her bed for about fifteen minutes. When I checked to see what she was doing, I found her sound asleep, a fistful of Tinker Toys in one hand and a wrinkled, moldy orange in the other. Bless her heart, she was trying; but cleaning up a room isn't too thrilling when you're three years old. Or when you're all grown up.

"Why is she so mad?" David asked Karen. The older children had come home and were standing around in the kitchen glancing sideways at the refrigerator.

"She's ticked off because the house is always such a mess," Karen said.

"I don't think it's so bad," John commented. "I've seen worse." I couldn't imagine where.

"She's probably mad because Daddy bawled her out the other night about not throwing things away," Susan said. "When she gets mad at Daddy, *we* have to clean the house." I hated to admit it, but Susan was right. And for a few days the children halfheartedly picked up their dirty clothes, put things in wastebaskets, and kept Augie from sleeping on their beds. I decided to start my spring cleaning by starting right. I was going to throw things away, just as my husband had suggested. Naturally, I was going to start with his stuff.

"I'm going to throw a lot of things away," I sang out gaily that evening as we finished clearing the table and Lee had picked up the paper. "I'm going to do it tonight." Lee nodded and continued to read. "I'll start with your side of the closet," I said in a loud voice. He swayed once, shot up from his chair, and ran to our bedroom, where he practically threw his body in front of the closet door. "Stop!" he yelled. "Don't do anything foolish."

"I'm not doing anything foolish," I said. "I'm only going to throw away things like you suggested; I'm going to start with these awful shirts you wear to work." Some of them had buttons hanging by a slender thread, pockets torn and weeping from the chest, patterns faded and washed away, and armpits wrinkled. These were his favorite shirts and the ones that screamed for the gentle, tender touch of a good homemaker. He had others but he chose to wear the ragged ones in public. "I'm going to get rid of these shirts," but before I could say "scat" he'd possessively gathered them up in his arms; to get them away from him, I would've had to wrench off an elbow. I turned to the closet again. Holding up a glum-looking piece of brown corduroy, screwed together by a broken zipper, I said, "Why do you still keep this old pair of trousers? I think I'll put them in the Goodwill box, but God knows what they will do with them. If they're washed one more time they'll dissolve."

"Well, don't wash them," Lee growled. Snatching the brown mess from my hands, he added them to his pile of shirts. "Those are my garden pants. They're like old friends. You don't go around donating old friends to the Goodwill." Well, I could think of a few, as Helen's image crossed my mind.

I turned to a stack of shoes on the closet floor. Now here was a real mess. Tangled in a stew of shoestrings were a dozen or so pairs of shoes, assorted as to style, color, and disrepair. "Take this old pair of hunting boots," I said, holding them up so he could see. "There is no way you can wear this pair of boots." The tongue was broken, the instep was cracked, and the soles were peeling from the bottom. "I've just broken those boots in," he shouted. "And *you* want to throw them away. God, woman, what are you thinking of?" I thought he was going to cry.

"I'm just doing as you suggested," I said sweetly. Sugar wouldn't melt. "Throwing things away." And I moved toward the top shelf on his side of the closet. As I reached up to pull down a large, ragged cowboy hat, a steellike grip came down on my wrist, nearly cracking the bone. "There's absolutely nothing up there to throw away," Lee said. The tips of his ears were turning white. My efforts were about to pay off. I could tell. "Hey, there," he said, releasing my wrist. The color was returning to his ears. "Let's forget this cleaning nonsense," and he caressed my shoulder. "We'll find something better than that to do. You shouldn't work so hard. Besides, the house looks fine to me. You deserve some fun in life. Come on, I bet I can beat you in gin rummy."

I hate to play gin rummy. But I hate cleaning a house worse. And besides, it was the best offer I'd had all night.

6

I'll Take Two of Everything You Have

I THINK IF I HAD a choice of profession in my next life, I'd be a door-to-door salesperson. I can't think of anything more exciting than peeking into people's houses when they didn't know I was coming. I wouldn't care if they bought anything or not—just catching Helen with her dust rag down would be commission enough for me. I loved having door-to-doors drop in because it was such a change of pace when someone spoke to me and didn't say "tee-tee" or "poo-poo." Lee thought they were a pain. When he was home, he was so rude he reduced them to pudding and sent most of them scurrying out of our yard before they could open up their portfolios. Not I! I welcomed them with open arms and could hardly wait for spring and the first invasion in our neighborhood.

"We're having company," I said to Claudia when I spied a salesman walking up our front sidewalk with two fat suitcases in his hands. "Be nice." Tidying my hair, I threw open the screen before Mr. Door-to-Door could even knock. My enthusiasm took him so much by surprise that he forgot what he was selling. The poor man had no way of knowing that I had only fifteen cents in my billfold and detailed instructions from my husband that if I bought anything from a traveling salesman it had better be something we needed. This kept

him safe in case someone dropped by peddling sailboats
or season tickets to the Kansas City Royals' baseball
games. Mr. Door-to-Door represented the Peaceful Rest
Company. As he admired Claudia, I admired his cemetery plots.

"What a sweet face," he smiled, tickling Claudia under the chin.

"It certainly looks grassy here," I complimented,
leafing through the colored photographs of well-kept
spaces surrounded by nodding daisies and peonies as big
as watermelons.

"How many children do you have?" he asked, handing me a slightly wrinkled purple bookmark with "Rest
in Peace" spelled out in sequins.

"Seven," I replied, and his eyebrows went straight to
his hairline as he ticked off the numbers in the back of
his head, positive he could unload a lot as large as two
city blocks in this single house. His hands were posi-
tively shaking as he whipped out an order blank, preparing to lay me away in a corner near a cow pasture.

"I'll have to talk to my husband," I said, sealing his
doom. He'd heard that one before, and knew how husbands felt about buying anything they couldn't eat on
the spot, fish with, or drive. Quietly gathering up his
glossies, contracts, and dreams of living off this one sale
for six months, he left me waiting for the next person to
swing off the sidewalk with his wares.

The day Lee came home and found three crates of
grapefruit in the kitchen was the day he told Augie that
if he didn't start attacking anyone with a pencil in his
hand, he could just start looking for someone else to provide dog room and board.

"Don't blame Augie," I said. "He wasn't even home
when they came. There was this man and woman in this
big, old beat-up truck, and they had four little children
with them and they said they had to get rid of the fruit

or their boss wouldn't pay them their wages and they made me such a good deal I couldn't pass it up. All that fresh fruit is good for us."

Lee reminded me that everyone in the family hated grapefruit but him and that I'd paid twice as much as our grocery store was charging. "I can't eat three crates of grapefruit before it spoils," he said. Bless his heart, he tried. I served him grapefruit for breakfast, lunch, and dinner and sent some to his office for coffee breaks. Putting it in the car in case he got hungry on the way home from work, I hung a couple over his workbench and stuck candles in them for his birthday. Finally, I told the children they could use what was left for bowling balls. As the crates began to dwindle, my courage was renewed. I took advantage of a wonderful opportunity to send fourteen underprivileged youths to Europe for summer study. I'd never even been to California myself, but through me and the dozens of magazine subscriptions I bought, these young people were to see the world.

"I can guarantee you they'll never make it to Paris," Lee said as he thumbed through the latest issue of *Jet Engine Mechanics*. "It's a gimmick to play on your sympathy. They don't really let them go to Europe."

"But he looked honest and studious," I said. "And he was so friendly and he had a cowlick and a Southern accent."

"Every supersalesman has a Southern accent," Lee scolded. "I'm surprised you didn't ask him to stay for dinner." I had but he'd leered, tugged on his cowlick, and said he only ate with widows.

For several days after buying every magazine published, I laid back and resisted the urge to advertise that I was home all day, come on, show me what you have. Claudia and I sat outside and watched the robins build their nests and Helen sweep her sidewalks. Helen

was busy cleaning her house for spring. Since I'd given
that up, it was enough for me to just sit and watch her
work herself to death.

Looking down the street, I saw a small blue Volkswagen shyly rolling down the block. In between stops
and starts, the driver laid her head on the steering
wheel and shuddered. She pulled up in front of Helen's
and stepped out of her car, only to scurry back quickly
when Helen thrust the broom at her stomach and shook
it threateningly. For a long, long time the poor lady sat
in front of Helen's house, and I thought maybe she'd
passed away, but slowly she started the car and turned
in our direction.

I watched as she took a deep breath, gathering courage to step out of her car. Glancing furtively across the
street at a glaring Helen, she trickled up our sidewalk
like a slow leak.

"Hi there," I called out. The woman jumped like
she'd been shot! "I'm sorry I bothered you," she called
out as she hurried back to her car. She was running by
now, and her suitcase bumped against her leg, causing
her to trip and crash into the side of the Volkswagen,
knocking off her. glasses and breaking her watch. She
burst into tears as I helped her to her feet, dusted her
off, and invited her in for a cup of coffee. "It's my first
day on the job," she admitted, "and you're the only person who's been nice to me. I'm quitting the minute I
leave here."

"Don't you even want to show me what you have?" I
asked eagerly. I felt so sorry for her that she could've
sold me horseshoes without half trying.

"Hell, no," she answered. "You can buy this stuff a
lot cheaper in the dime store." Obviously, the decision to
resign had made her fearless, and the two of us had a
grand time talking about the city council, the school
system, and our families. I discovered she'd been a bar-

tender, and she asked me who the witch was sweeping her sidewalk. Before she left she told me she was going right down and get her old job back, and if I'd drop in some afternoon she'd fix me up with the best Margarita in town—on the house—and she gave Claudia tiny little sample lipsticks, which she promptly ate, and Helen came right over the minute her car pulled from the curb and said I was a fool for letting every Tom, Dick, and Harry come into our house without checking at the Chamber of Commerce first to see if they had a license to sell.

But even Helen had fallen under the spell of one of our local door-to-doors and she didn't bother to check to see if he had a license either. He was the first thing our entire neighborhood looked for in the spring. Phooey on robins; who needed them? We had Mr. Door-to-Door. All he had to do was flash a gorgeous smile in my direction, and I bought cleaning fluids, mops, toothbrushes, and kitchen cleanser by the bushel. So did Helen.

"Spring has officially arrived," she told me happily on the telephone one morning. "He's here. I saw his car turn the corner down by the Mannings'. He's coming. He's really coming," she sang out.

"Do I have time to give myself a home permanent?" I asked. She told me she didn't think so because he was headed my way at that very minute. "Don't forget to tell him to stop over here," she said before she hung up. I had no time to get ready for him but it didn't matter how I looked. He made me feel like a queen.

"My, you're stunning this morning," he said as I opened the screen and his thirty-two beauties lit up my life. I was wearing a smudged blouse with two buttons missing, a pair of patched blue jeans, and bedroom slippers, and Claudia was nailed to my side like a third leg. Feeling like Elizabeth Taylor, I moved back so he could come into the house. Stepping gracefully over a rotted grapefruit, he pretended not to notice the pile of underwear on the couch. "How tastefully your house is decorated," he said with a catch in his voice. "Why, it's like a castle. What a lucky man your husband is . . . ," and he let the words fade away, so choked up with emotion he led me to believe his own home was a pit and his wife a slattern who slept until noon and ran about all night while he stayed home with the children. I truly thought he'd sacrifice every brush in his bag if he could trade places with Lee for a week. And he didn't lose his composure when Claudia carried away all of his giveaway combs but smiled happily and sold me fifteen jars of silver polish. And I had no silver.

Helen admitted to me later she had about a dozen brooms, all still in cellophane, stacked in her closet, and Lee and Ray threatened to turn him in to the police if they ever caught him hanging around the neighborhood.

But they never did because they never saw Mr. Door-to-Door. He came only when the men were gone, and somehow he knew when they weren't home. He didn't have a Southern accent either, come to think of it.

7

A Pretty Face Doesn't Mean a Thing Unless It Can Cook

WE WERE CONSTANTLY confronted by sweet, well-meaning spinsters who fawned on us as we lined up our seven in a front pew of the Presbyterian Church, where the minister could help us keep an eye on them. "Aren't big families nice," they commented as they watched Claudia spitting up on my one and only Sunday dress, Amy tearing up the visitor cards, and David trying to rip off the collection plate. "How proud you must be," they said. You bet we were proud—proud that we *got* them all there, buttoned and jockeyed and zippered into seven pairs of matching socks. Now mine didn't match, but the kids looked swell.

And we *were* proud, especially around income-tax season. When Uncle Sam knocked on our door, tall hat in hand, he handed *us* a check. We waited breathlessly for the government to send us that money. Ours was surely the first tax return to hit Washington, D.C. Horns were still sounding at New Year's Eve celebrations, but Lee had our income-tax forms made out, signed, and mailed.

I gathered our little deductions about me and said softly, "Wait until Daddy gets his tax money back and then we'll buy . . ."

New shoes for Amy, because her little curled-up toes were beginning to look unnatural and very cramped.

A Brownie beanie for Mary, so she could take her rightful place in the Brownie ring with pride.

Haircuts for John and David, so that I could send them to school without danger of having them sent back—or renamed Joan and Doris by the teacher.

A haircut for poor, shaggy Augie-Doggie, because he was beginning to scratch a lot and dog hair was appearing in the soup dishes.

A new garden hose to replace the one poor, shaggy Augie-Doggie chewed to pieces when he had a scratching fit.

A mute for John's cornet, so he'd be allowed to practice in the house on cold days instead of in the garage. Not even Harry James could triple-tongue with stiff gums.

A membership in the YWCA for Karen, so she could attend junior-high dances without having to ask for ticket money from a father who expected at least three references for each boy in the ninth grade.

Money to replace the bike tire David had slashed in order to hear the "whooooosh" made by escaping air.

Money to replace the pancake flopper I bent when I encouraged David never, never to slash anything for any reason ever again.

A couple of new stereo records for Susan, so she could substitute one when her Dad yelled, "If I hear that damn song one more time I'm going to smash every Beach Boy in the house."

A new bed for Claudia, as her present hand-me-down, six times used, was held together by spit and spearmint.

A new mink coat for mother? Probably not.

Group hearing tests for the children to see why they

couldn't hear "I need help with the dishes" but could hear a candy sack rattle three rooms away.

A hearing test for Lee, who couldn't seem to pick up the sounds of "Why can't we carpet the bathroom?" but could hear Ray whisper to Helen that he was planning to sell his motorboat.

Nine life jackets to put in a silly motorboat.

A night out on the town for Mom and Dad. Blow the whole works. Steak, a glass or two of wine, and a double feature (with buttered popcorn) at the local theater.

Gad, it was like the Christmas Club in April! Others complained of high taxes and the greedy government, while we sat around with complacent smiles on our faces. We kissed our seven little deductions as they slept in their little torn pajamas and scrambled bunk beds.

As the mother of a large family, I was either adored or treated as though I were on the wrong side of a gang war. Each of the children had a different way of expressing love for me. Some ways were subtle, some very outspoken, and some were found under layers of dirt. But they were there; they had to be. Why else would I wash fourteen dozen towels a day, pick catsup spots off the wall, volunteer to be a den mother, go on vacation with seven children, eat in the school cafeteria on Parents' Day, spend 75 percent of my waking hours hovering over a potty chair making funny noises, miss a big neighborhood tea party because of a bad case of chicken pox that wasn't even mine, and sometimes go behind the bathroom door to cry because I felt tired, lonely, and put upon. Oh, I knew the ways and I didn't have to be told.

As each child approached a certain stage he or she "saw" me in a different way. Through their eyes it didn't matter how old I was, how tall, or how much lipstick I wore. My maternal looks didn't mean a thing. When they were infants, different parts of me were more important than others . . . especially at mealtime. They couldn't have cared less about my facial features; and it didn't matter if I were strikingly beautiful or homely as a mud fence; all they were interested in was that I appear on schedule with the right equipment. I didn't doubt that I was loved, because their contentment was so burpingly obvious.

To toddling Claudia, my image meant fast legs and quick hands. She checked up on my interest in her by running through the living room stark naked, waving a banner of poopy diapers when we had important company, unscrewing the controls on the television, tossing a block at a tiny playmate, choking the cat, eating a sponge, or eating a penny, while listening very hard to see if I would be there in time to stop her from doing something awful. When I did and shook a "no-no" finger at her, she was content: she knew she was loved. She rewarded me by sleeping all night and calling glamorous photographs of svelte fashion models "Mommy."

It was natural for me to be concerned when Amy cried on her first day of kindergarten, but underneath I was a bit pleased too. This helped later on when I felt the pain of being replaced in her affections by singing games, ABC's, new friends, and the teacher. Her love turned into grubby crayon artwork that portrayed me as a straight-haired crone with no teeth, or a fat fairy with bobbling breasts and tears falling down my chubby cheeks; or else I was pictured in a scarlet shimmy, with a sinister grin and a bottle of beer. I knew Amy loved me because I was the central figure in every picture she drew.

Imaginative Mary did so wish for a queen in her castle instead of a cornflake-type mother like me. With a best friend, Robin (whose own mother was much younger and much slimmer and a pretty blonde), Mary sat at the dining-room table eating cookies and milk after school. The two of them watched as I hotfooted across the kitchen floor with a greasy casserole in my hand and an ugly look on my face. I knew Mary loved me when Robin got pinched because she said I was fat and cross.

As a fourth grader, David saw me as nurse, knee washer, elbow mender, costume maker, cookie baker, noodle cooker, and Augie feeder. I was the shadow that put him to bed at night and woke him in the morning. He was more interested in finding out how our neighbor's dog had puppies than he was in exploring how I looked. I don't really think he cared how I looked. I was as comfortable and common as his favorite pair of rotten tennis shoes. I knew I was loved, though, when he graciously allowed me to be the first to know that he'd thrown up on his pillow at 2 A.M.

John chose not to see me at all. Especially in mixed company. He often crossed the street to avoid meeting me face to face. John's best defense against showing any sort of love was to ignore me completely. Days went by without meaningful conversation. I'd put in twelve good years on raising a son who said good morning and good evening with nothing in between. I searched his eyes for something that might indicate love, found nothing, and then discovered that he'd saved his allowance for six weeks to buy me a small transistor radio so that I could have music in every room of the house as I worked. I needed no canned music at that point. I carried the lilting melody of my son's love in my heart.

Susan and Karen, too, preferred that I remain invisible. But they remembered me. Because they volunteered me to chaperone a junior-high dance as well as to make all the relishes. When I appeared in the hallway of their school, they brushed by me like strangers and giggled nervously until I'd passed their lockers. As long as I had a dollar bill pinned on my bosom and a plate of hot tacos handy, they didn't comment on my looks. But their love was not far away, and that love was apparent when they came home fifteen minutes before curfew, spontaneously cleaned their rooms, did their own laundry, called from school to let me know they'd made the honor roll, and let me read what their **friends** had written in their school memory books.

The biggest advantage of having so many children *was* the love, of course, but it also meant I got a lot of presents for Mother's Day. It was my favorite holiday.

8

Dust and Shut Up. . . . It's Mother's Day

POSSIBLY WE WERE the only people on the block who celebrated Mother's Day with a vengeance. Everyone else went to visit relatives or out to the Interstate restaurant for a nice buffet. At our house Mother's Day started directly after dawn and lasted until my exhausted children dropped into their beds. They'd spent one entire twenty-four-hour period trying to be "good" and it had been very hard on them. It had been hard on me too, because I had to live up to the image I knew they expected. "I'll never make it through the day," I groaned, thinking of past Mother's Days when I'd found six newborn kittens in my sewing basket and received a half-dozen turkey skewers as my only gifts. "I never know what to expect." Lee took my hand and wisely told me I should be happy to know I was worth staging a celebration for. He could say that; usually on Father's Day we went fishing and had a picnic.

The second Sunday in May was circled in red on the calendar three weeks in advance. When a family shopping trip was organized and I wasn't invited, I pretended ignorance. I told them to run along. I took the time they were gone to do my nails, read a love story, and call Helen to find out what they were going to do on Mother's Day.

70

"I ordered flowers for his mother, my mother, and me and charged them to Ray; the children are adding to my china, and we'll spend the day cleaning the patio." Well organized, efficient, clear-cut but with no juice, I thought. As I said good-bye I heard a car in the driveway. The children and Lee had returned, and I knew without looking that Lee's face would be bright red and the first thing he'd reach for was a cold beer. Shopping alone with the children always made him thirsty and slightly dopey for about three hours. The children's cheeks were flushed too, and as they ran from the car to their rooms, Karen taking Claudia and Amy led by Susan, they crossed in front of me and whispered in very loud voices, entirely for my benefit, "Don't tell Mommy what you bought."

"I not know what it is," Claudia complained as she was pulled across the floor by a determined Karen. I discovered later she'd cried for a full ten minutes because she wasn't allowed to buy Tinker Toys so Mommy would have something to play with.

Lee told me this was probably the last time he'd ever take any of them shopping again as long as he lived, and next Mother's Day I could order flowers and we'd go out to the Interstate for dinner. He said that every year, and every year I said it sounded fine, but we never did it. Following his second beer his face regained its normal color, and he explained that John and David had fought right in front of the cologne counter, squirting each other with demonstrators, causing the cologne clerk's blood pressure to peak at 205 and them to stink so badly that one older lady, terribly allergic to perfumes, became so choked up someone called an ambulance. Susan, he said, had been caught reading every dirty magazine hidden in the back of the store and had to be firmly persuaded that I wouldn't appreciate a subscription to a magazine featuring nude men as centerfolds. Personally, I thought that idea beat turkey skewers by a mile.

And with dark eyes snapping (and a hint of humor around the edges), he described being the focus of attention while sitting on the floor in the middle of shopper traffic and replacing Amy's shoes and stockings while everyone stood around, watched, and clapped. "I did this three times," he said.

"Why didn't you have Karen do it?"

"Hell, she was chasing boys, with Claudia screaming at her heels. And Mary got lost, and for a minute I thought she'd gone with the ambulance. I didn't have time to get you a present myself. I'm sorry."

"That's all right," I assured him. "I'm not *your* mother." And when he hugged me tight with both arms, we agreed it was much better this way.

Mother's Day arrived, and the early Sunday morning quiet was shoved out the window as I heard muffled voices, scufflings, and scurryings in the kitchen. I knew what was happening. Someone was spilling orange juice, dropping eggshells, and burning brown rot on the bottom of my expensive electric fry pan. I was right. John and David were fixing breakfast. Karen and Susan wanted nothing to do with the kitchen. They helped in there every day, so on Mother's Day they, too, took a sabbatical and turned the cooking over to their brothers while they helped the three little girls dress.

"Damn!" I heard John say as something crashed to the floor.

"You'd better be quiet; Mom will hear you and you know how mad she gets when we swear." David's voice carried down the hallway accompanied by the awful smell of burning bread.

"Why don't you go see what they're doing." I poked Lee, who was gently snoring beside me. "John's swearing and David's burning the house down."

"If it gets too bad they'll call the fire department." He turned over to sleep some more. Tossing the covers off and exposing him to the crisp morning breeze, I told him that was exactly what I was afraid of. "I want no strange firemen running around our house while I'm wearing your pajama tops and you're wearing *no* pajamas. Let's get dressed and go eat. We have to do it sooner or later."

Ordinarily, I don't tiptoe into the kitchen and grin at eggshells on the floor, but this morning I swallowed the urge to scream out loud and scrunched my way across the room and sat down at the table, nodding hello to a wilted tulip stuck in a water glass. And as the boys hovered over me saying, "Do you like it?" "Is it good?" I was served black bacon and runny eggs.

"I like it and it is good," I gulped, noticing that neither boy had washed his hands.

"Then why isn't Dad eating?" David pointed at his dad, who was sitting with a sheepish smile and glass of orange juice in his hand.

"It isn't Father's Day," Lee said.

"Is it time for presents yet?" Amy asked impatiently. She was ready for the important stuff. She'd eaten half a green pepper and a banana for breakfast and was squirming because I was dawdling over my eggs.

"Not yet," Karen said. "We have to pick up the house first."

"Why?" Susan wanted to know. Susan had no problems with picking up. She simply didn't do it, and she saw no reason to start just because it was Mother's Day.

"Mom doesn't want to open presents in a mess. Don't argue. Do it!" Karen seemed to be in control so I didn't interfere with her motherly bossiness. Surprisingly enough, there were no fights about who was going to clear the table, scrape the black bacon into the disposal, or who was going to vacuum. John was going to vacuum. "But I'm not going to dust," he said. "No matter what you do to me, I'm not going to dust."

"Dust!" Karen hissed. "And shut up. It's Mother's Day." I pretended not to see him take a swipe at her with the heavy end of the rag; and, as John gave in to someone he could ordinarily intimidate with a grasshopper, I also pretended not to watch as he shook the dust rag around the room like a samurai sword. I had visions of my one and only antique vase ending its life in a million expensive pieces; I prayed he would remember that delicate things were treated with the same respect and tender care given a newborn puppy. He did, and nothing was broken.

"Is it time for presents?" A pink bow peeped from behind Amy's back. She was ready.

"No one emptied the garbage," Karen said. "We can't have presents until that's done. Mom doesn't want to look at smelly eggs when she opens presents."

"Don't look at me." John put both hands in the air to show he was done with woman's work. "I dusted. I'm not going to dust *and* empty garbage." Lee emptied the garbage. It was Mother's Day.

"Now is it time for presents?" Amy asked eagerly.

"Now!" I said. "It's time. I can hardly wait." I smelled strong perfume, and a gigantic pair of rhinestone earrings glittered in the morning sunlight. I was handed a bundt pan and a purse-sized plastic pencil sharpener. A puzzled Claudia gave me a meat thermometer, and Amy's pink bow covered a canvas tote bag with a smiling green frog on it. "You take it shopping, Mommy."

John's gift was a small, thumbed-through paperback entitled *328 Corny Jokes for Convulsive Conversation.*

"This is a real good book, Mom. It's funny." He seemed envious and reluctant to part with it. I thanked him and told him I could hardly wait to read it. Lee brought out a large leafy Boston fern, and I knew I would soon have another plant death on my conscience. But I could always tell it jokes. At least it would die happy.

"Here's my present, Mom," David said, thrusting a paper sack tied in twine in front of me. He stood back proudly as I opened it. Sniffing back a catch in my throat, I read the inscription on the rather homely ceramic plaque he'd given me:

> To one who bears the sweetest name,
> And adds luster to the same
> Long life to her,
> For there's no other, Who takes the place
> Of My Dear Mother!

The author was anonymous and the price tag still clung to the back; but to me it was the most beautiful work of art and poetry in the world. It was something I would treasure forever.

Later that evening as I sat, surrounded by pencil sharpener, meat thermometer, and bundt pan, wearing cologne that was strong enough to drop a race horse with one whiff, both ears pinched with rhinestones, I read and reread 328 corny jokes to a droopy Boston fern. Amy crawled on my lap, hugged my neck, sighed, snuggled down into my arms, and said, "Just think, Mommy, you have all this good stuff and *us* too. You're so lucky."

And do you know, I think she was right.

9
How Important Is This Dance?

OVER THE YEARS, I'd grown used to whipping up a few dozen cookies at the tail end of the day because John failed to tell me he'd promised to feed the entire boy-scout troop; I was adept at turning Lee's underwear into a bunny suit for Mary five minutes before her performance at PTA; and it was nothing for me to quickly fashion a pompom from the innards of the Montgomery Ward's catalogue for Susan's pep rally. I expected to do these things. Probably, I thought, it was the reason I was put on earth in the first place.

I tried explaining this to Lee as he prowled the house looking for signs and smells of supper while I hemmed a pair of dress pants for David, who'd been chosen three weeks earlier to usher at the elementary spring band concert. David had known full well he had no fancy pants and that he'd have to borrow his brother's. He didn't mention it until fifteen minutes before he was due to stand at the door, but I shrugged it off and sewed as fast as I could.

"Will they ever stop waiting until the last minute?" Lee grumbled.

"Of course they will," I lied. "When they are in high school they'll have long-range goals and learn to plan ahead. At least that's what the counselor said." Karen was due to enter high school in the fall, and I'd been pumped full of buoyant promises by a man counselor who I decided later had probably received his doctorate in needlepoint. He didn't know a damn thing about teenaged girls.

He'd leaned back in his chair, stroked his chin academically, and, as I explained that we were raising a rather large family, he nodded sympathetically and said, "Don't worry, Mother, I think I can get her a scholarship to a good college."

"Shouldn't we get her through high school first?" I asked.

"Ahhhhhhh, we must plan ahead," and he yanked his chair around to stare me straight in the eye. And that's when he gave me all of the baloney about young people being responsible when they entered high school. "In fact, you should be seeing definite signs of dependability by now. Trust me, Mother," he said as he glanced slyly at his impressive diploma on the wall as if to say, "Can't you see which of us is the smart one in this room?" I think it might have been me because he handed me applications for scholarships that Karen could receive if (1) she was the child of non-English-speaking Russian immigrants; (2) either parent was a deceased veteran of World War Two; and (3) either parent was spending time in a federal prison. I came away from our meeting feeling as if I had holes in my underwear and that possibly from that moment on, cookie baking, bunny suits, pompoms, and hemming pants were going to be pushovers.

And I was right. One afternoon following my visit to the counselor, Karen walked into the kitchen where I was boxing a bud vase for Helen's birthday and wondering how I could rearrange it so it would look terribly expensive instead of dime store, and casually flipped a verbal grenade right in my lap.

"I've been invited to the junior-high graduation dance," she said.

"Wonderful," I smiled. It always makes a mother feel good to know her children are having fun. "Who asked, and when did he ask?"

"Oh," she said tiredly, "it's Robert and I got the invitation about two weeks ago."

"Why didn't you tell me sooner?" I screamed.

"You get so excited, Mother, that's why I didn't tell you. It doesn't matter anyway. I can't go."

"Of course you can go. Or is there something wrong with Robert?"

"Robert's fine. In fact, he's double fine. I can't go, that's all," and she got this hangdog fifteen-year-old look that plainly said, *I loathe life, this house, the entire family, and myself.* "I don't have anything to wear."

"But you do," I said, reminding her of the lovely dancing dress we'd bought within the past year for a Y-teen party. Though we'd probably spent fourteen hours straight looking for it and a week's salary paying for it, the dress had been worth it. She'd looked so pretty. As far as I knew, the dress had been put back into its clothing bag to stand in her closet, like a gorgeous princess, untouched, unworn, and unloved. This was its chance to return to the social world in all its shimmering glory.

"I can't wear *that* dress, Mom," she whined. "It's a formal dance. I won't be the only one there who has legs showing. Everyone else is wearing a long dress."

"Be different," I said. "Don't be a sheep."

"I won't go if my legs stick out!" She was looking hangdoggier with every passing minute. Giving in, I sighed and said I supposed that I could make a long dress. "We'll shop for a pattern and material this weekend."

"The dance is this weekend," she said softly. She was barely breathing.

"I can't make a dress in two days." I was on the point of collapse just thinking about it. Lord, it took me two days to work up enough courage to even approach my sewing machine. The poor thing had a backward bobbin and if I told it that I expected to make a full-fledged party dress in forty-eight hours, it would spin itself to death. "Why didn't you tell me sooner?" I resisted the urge to shake her pretty shoulders until her pretty head fell off.

"I forgot."

"Who is going to break this news to your father?" I asked wearily. I would've rather walked straight up to a madman and kissed him directly on the mouth than approach my husband for money for another new party dress.

"You do it, Mom. He likes you."

Not that well, I told her. I knew the subtle ways of getting men to do something you wanted them to do—I'd read them in magazines—but I didn't have the time or money to run out and buy champagne and red roses. I had no candles without teethmarks and even if I had all of these things stuck away in a cupboard somewhere, the chances of my arranging a quiet little corner for a private and seductive tête-à-tête were practically impossible. I'd just have to do what I always did. Use the direct method. "I'll have to have your billfold," I told Lee when he came in the door that night.

"What now!" he moaned. "Is it the plumbing? I can fix that," and he ran to get a ratchet. "Is it the light switch? I can fix that," and he ran to get a screwdriver. "Is it new dining-room drapes again," and he prepared to say no.

"It's *your* daughter," I said. "She needs a new dress for the junior-high dance."

"I just bought her one six weeks ago. Why am I buying another? I've worn my suit two hundred sixty-five times. Can't she wear a dress twice?" I patiently explained that the dress was nearly a year old; and it was short, and she needed long. "There's a big difference," I guaranteed. Confused by the entire situation, Lee handed over his billfold and I took two aspirin because it always gave me a terrible headache when I had to beg for money. I tried to hype myself to deal with the raw conflict I knew was ahead when I voluntarily went shopping with a child old enough to read price tags and designer labels.

"We will find a dress," I said out loud as Karen and I drove downtown the next morning. "We will *not* argue. We will *not* fight. We *will* find a dress."

"We'll *never* find a dress." Karen slumped in the seat beside me and had a hateful look in her eye. "I won't go to the silly dance. We'll never find a formal that costs nine ninety-eight." Drilled into her head since she was an infant was her father's philosophy that anything costing over ten dollars was obscene, illegal, or fattening.

"Daddy wants you to have a pretty dress," I said, trying to cheer her up. "And so do I. Just remember, he isn't with us and I have the credit cards. Do you have on clean underwear?" She snorted twice and gave me "that" look. The look that meant: this mother knows nothing about style, this mother, who wears polyester pantsuits and low-heeled shoes, this mother, who insists on eating lunch in a restaurant with a salad bar instead of in a dive with sawdust on the floor, this mother, who was trying to take over her life again. I was to get "that" look many times throughout the day.

Parking the car in front of a conventional, modern, stable-looking dress shop with clean windows, I was happy to note its display was tastefully decorated with crispy dresses, Schiffli-embroidered blouses, and pull-on pants. A dash of real daring splashed out in the form of perforated, open-toed wedgies.

"I'm not going in there," Karen rebelled, pulling

back as I opened the door to shove her inside. "There's nothing in there I want. We'd be wasting our time. This store is for old ladies," and, dragging about four feet behind me, she pretended she was invisible.

"You never know until you've looked." I pointed her in the direction of the back of the store. On long racks were about fifteen or twenty perfectly nice long dresses, each with a proper neckline and decent price. I drew one from the rack and held it before her. "See how dainty it is, how sweet?"

"I won't try it on," she sulked. "I hate it." Strike store number one.

A variety store, well known for discount prices, was next door. It had a crowded corner devoted to women's wear and, mixed in with tacky gauze blouses and cheap twill jeans, were ugly, artificial funeral sprays and large canisters of Planter's peanuts. A chipped manikin with no left hand, wearing a rather nice full-length waltzing gown with pink piping and elastic waist, stood next to sheets and pillowcases. The manikin was also wearing a pair of linty black-felt bedroom slippers on her feet. "No, thank you," Karen giggled. Strike store number two.

She practically jogged through stores three, four, five, and six. We'd covered eighteen blocks, visited half a dozen stores, and she hadn't even been inside a dressing room. She came close once. A soft little wisp with eight yards of material in the skirt and about four inches of net on top caught her eye.

"Ooooooooooooh," she cooed. "I like this one."

"Sure you do," I said. The total price (without tax) was $159. "There's no need to even slip that one from its hanger," I said. After all, I reminded her, she wasn't accepting an Academy Award, only attending a junior-high dance.

It was my turn to pull back when we went through the door of a chic boutique. The rafters were blistered

with hot rock music, and the aisles squeezed full of tight
jeans and scanty stretch tops. The clerk, wearing fringe,
a headband, fourteen turquoise rings on grimy fingers,
had a cloud of funny-smelling smoke encircling her
head. "A formal," she hooted. "What's a formal, big
mama?" Definitely strike store number seven.

"We're nearly out of places to look," I told Karen
when we stepped back on the sidewalk. I was bushed,
and as far as I could tell we were going to have to find
this dress in a hardware store, a dry cleaner, a book-
store, a savings and loan, the utility company, or a
pharmacy. There seemed to be nothing else left. Was I
going to have to go back and give in to that little $159
number? And if I did, how would I explain it to Lee? I
decided I couldn't. My feet hurt, my head ached, my
throat was dry, and I'd seen enough satin and lace to
last me a lifetime. "How important is this dance?" I
asked Karen.

Oh, well, there was one store left, impressively
dowdy in decor. Karen shuffled in the door swearing
she'd never find anything in *here,* and I led her toward
the back, where I'd spied a young moderns department.
The salesperson was under thirty, had clear skin and
clean fingernails. She didn't pounce on us but let us
browse, and when I suggested a pale yellow, semi-sensa-
tional, reasonably priced classic gown with just enough
bare skin showing to satisfy a fifteen-year-old but not
enough to shock a mother, and Karen agreed to try it
on, she winked as I bowed my head in silent prayer.

A few minutes later Karen emerged from the dressing room looking like an elegant butterfly, if you didn't
count striped tube socks and dirty sneakers. Twirling
before the mirror she said, "I like it!" I breathed a quiet
"Thank You, Lord," and the salesperson clapped her
hands. "Wrap it up! Quick!" I told her. "Before she

changes her mind." And the fastest purchase in the history of man was made at that moment.

After we'd added a warm wrap, suitable shoes, long slip, earrings, necklace, and evening purse, we'd shot the $159 mark by a mile but I decided I could explain that to Lee, especially after he took one look at her.

If I do say so myself, Karen looked smashing.

10

There's Nothing to Do at My House When It Rains

I HAPPEN TO LIKE children better than I do rutabagas, spiders, dust, gin, and whisker burns, but even I had to admit that when school ended that May, I didn't run around in the streets shouting hurrah, hurrah my children will be home for three full months. I did, however, sit at our kitchen window for a few select moments every morning. When I looked outside at the deep quiet of our neighborhood, I saw no one clutching paper sacks, hurrying to catch the bus. I watched the early-morning summer roses stand up tall with dew on their lips before they were squashed down by eager bare feet, and Augie and his various dog pals stretch in the sunlight as they prepared for a rip-roaring day with their freedom-bound friends.

During the school year, Augie was my closest companion. He spent the majority of his day sitting on my feet. Certainly Claudia was home, but she was much too young to interest Augie and she often bit his tail. Amy wasn't into dogs; a cat lover, she respected Augie, simply because he was the type of dog that demanded respect, but she could sometimes be found forcing his mouth open with both chubby hands, counting his teeth. He took his chances with me and followed me faithfully as I did my daily chores.

84

During the summer months, he totally snubbed me. He definitely wasn't interested in trailing behind a grown-up lady who had her hands elbow deep in sandy carpets, damp bath towels, and crusty closets. Such commonplace activities couldn't come close to the hours spent running through sprinklers on newly seeded lawns with John and David or tromping through Helen's prized peonies, hunting lost gold mines down by the river or stealing someone's golf ball off the ninth hole at the country-club course. I tried not to let it bother me, as I told myself that a dog wasn't much of a best friend for a mother anyway. "My day will come again," I whispered softly as I watched boys and dog go down the sidewalk. "My day will come." And I knew it would.

"In about two months," I told Helen, who'd dropped in to tell me she'd signed her two oldest children up for summer violin lessons, "I'm positive the boys will be tired of vacation and they'll roll around, bored to death, and they'll look to me for guidance. I can hear them now. 'What'll we do, Mom, what'll we do?' Don't ask me, I'll say; ask Augie-Doggie."

"You'd let a *dog* plan your children's summer?" Helen gasped as if I'd stuck her with a pin.

"Why not?" and, pouring another cup of coffee for the two of us, I removed the telephone from Mary's hand and reassured the operator that no, we didn't really need an ambulance; it was only my little girl playing make-believe. "You see, Helen," I continued. "I really and truly think children should have time in the summer to have fun, get bored, cry, laugh, and go to bed at an early hour."

She could hardly believe her ears. "I can't imagine," she said, "that you'd cold-bloodedly let your children spend the summer resorting to their own devices. I have every minute planned. Sarah Ann will take tap, ballet, swim, acrobatics, pastels, sewing, and gourmet cook-

ing—not to mention violin. Matthew Allen too will have
swim and violin along with basketball, football, soccer,
karate and foreign-language camps. We'll not see him
all summer." Lucky you, I thought.

"Poor Marilyn Lorraine is too young to register for
anything, though," Helen said in a disappointed voice.
"I'm not sure what I'll do with her."

It wasn't long before I found out.

In Nebraska, farmers love rainy days, as do local
birds, frogs, and lawns. Everyone in this heartland country was grateful when we had a period of two or more
days of summer rain. I was the only one I knew who stood
around wishing it would dry up, for goodness' sake, and
this was because I was the mother of several children
who had no violin lessons or karate camps to go to.

Poor Helen discovered that when it was wet outside,
four-year-old Marilyn Lorraine turned into a group
when confined inside. Her mouth rang out like a chorus;
two busy hands suddenly became fourteen mischievous
ones; a fluffy pink-and-white bedroom turned into a
prison cell; and the teddy bears on her bed might as well
have had rabies, Marilyn Lorraine wouldn't touch them.
Helen had only one thing left to do. She sent her over to
my house. "They won't even know you're there," I'm
sure she said, squatting down to tie a shiny red ribbon
in Marilyn Lorraine's hair. "Just slip inside the door
when no one is looking and mingle."

I recognized right away this wasn't my child. Wasn't
she wearing a ribbon at 9:30 A.M.? Most of the children
living at our house were still sitting around in their pajamas. I saw no reason to insist they dress in real
clothing just to punch each other out.

"Hello," Marilyn Lorraine smiled when I answered
the door. Quick as a flash she removed her yellow
slicker and white rainboots, and left an opened umbrella
to puddle in the foyer. "I can spend the whole day with
you. Mama said."

"Marvelous!"

"There's nothing to do at my house when it rains," she said, shaking my hand politely.

"Oh," I shook back, "we're having a circus, a sixteen-piece band is coming and Captain Kangaroo said he might drop by."

"Mama told me I needn't be too careful because everything at your house is broken anyway," and little Marilyn Lorraine stepped into what to her was a paradise of jelly juice and paper wads. I don't care what Helen thought; I wasn't ready for organized play on rainy days. I did let Karen and Susan experiment with my makeup, warned the boys not to pinch Marilyn Lorraine, and turned my head when they dressed a surprised Augie up in my best sweater set and pearls and tried to get him to wear high heels. But I didn't tell *anyone* they could talk an innocent Marilyn Lorraine into shedding her clothing and playing "G-string, G-string, who's got the G-string?"

"What will her mother think?" I scolded as I retied the red ribbon in our tiny guest's hair. Her face was flushed and her eyes were as bright as stars.

"I liked that game," she giggled hysterically. "I'm going to tell my daddy about it when he comes home. He likes games too."

"I wouldn't, honey," I told her, visualizing Ray's attempts to incorporate the same idea into our next neighborhood block party. I diverted her attention with a big cookie. These cookies were my rainy-day specialty. Instead of wasting all that precious time methodically oozing them out with a rusty cutter, I simply slashed a few long strokes with a knife through the dough and in a matter of seconds had dozens of large square ones. Who said a cookie had to be round anyway?

"This is a funny cookie," Marilyn Lorraine said, turning it around and around in her hand suspiciously. "My mama doesn't make funny cookies."

"You have a dull mother," I muttered behind my hand. As the long afternoon wore on and on and on, I decided she also had a smart mother. A smart mother who was more than likely propped up for the afternoon on a couch reading a book, enjoying my soap opera and relaxing to the pitter-patter of raindrops outside. I was cooped up inside and found no pleasure in the gallop-galloping going on about me.

"Stop running through this house at once," I shouted as eight invisible ponies darted behind chairs, over couches, and under my toes. Marilyn Lorraine was breathing hard and had lost her red ribbon.

"Giddy-ap!" she cried in perfect abandonment and, whinnying with all her might, she swung one arm very high and hit Lee square in the stomach as he walked in the room. He was slightly damp, a bit cross, and very startled to be greeted with a pummeling in his own home. "Whoa!" He reached out, grabbed her, and held tight. "You know better than to run in the house. Slow down or I'll send you to your room."

"You can't send her to her room, Daddy," Mary said brightly. "She doesn't have one."

"My God, you're right!" Lee said, taking a closer look at the arm he was clutching. Two round eyes looked fearfully into his. "She doesn't belong to us. Who *does* she belong to?"

"That's Marilyn Lorraine, Daddy," Amy said. "She's been here all day." Marilyn Lorraine trembled in her patent-leather shoes.

"My mama said I could stay," she said, her underlip quivering ever so slightly.

"Of course you can stay, honey," Lee hugged, and picking her up under one arm, Amy in the other, and with Claudia squealing in delight behind him, he danced into the dining room looking much like a papa walrus. "And you can have dinner with us, too."

"Will we have square stuff?" she asked. "I don't think I can stay if it's going to taste like the funny cookie."

I forced a smile and told her we were having macaroni and cheese. "Mom's macaroni isn't square," David explained. "It's lumpy and the cheese is stretchy but it tastes real good." Marilyn Lorraine nodded her head and decided it might be worth taking a chance for. "My mama makes broccoli soup and fish when it rains. I like macaroni better."

"I'm glad I don't have to eat at your house," Mary sighed happily. "And I won't let the boys poke you with a fork either. You can sit by Daddy. That's the safe chair." At bedtime Marilyn Lorraine went home. She'd had a busy day and as I watched her little yellow slicker disappear into the house across the street I reached down and picked up a shiny red object curled up under the rug. "Uhhhhhm, I wonder," I asked, giving Lee a wicked wink, "if a red ribbon would make a good G-string?"

"You might give it a try," he winked back.

I've always said there's not a helluva lot to do on a rainy summer evening after the company goes home.

11
Who Said a Zoo Was Fun?

IT WAS A QUIET SUNDAY. Lee was sitting peacefully in the living room, cold drink in hand, dish of peanuts by his side, contented smile on his face, and a 13–13 tie major-league baseball game on television. He was in Father's Heaven and all was right with his world. There had been four home runs to cheer, two death-defying leaps in left field, a few fights with the third-base umpire, and a hyperventilating fan had been carried out by the rescue squad. The game was about to go into extra innings. "This is no way for you to spend a Sunday," I said, clicking off the TV as a pinch hitter stepped to the plate with bases loaded. "You shouldn't sit here all alone like this. It's Sunday. A day for family fun. Let's go to the zoo."

Lee feels the same way about zoos as he does about fabric stores, cute little tea shops, and high-school musicals; but Sunday, I reminded him, is Family Day all over the world and he was our Father. The children and I were excited. Well, not all were excited. Karen thought she was much too old to accompany us anywhere other than a dim cocktail lounge. (She'd never been to one but was looking forward to it.) Susan claimed she didn't have anything decent to wear to a zoo, and John was upset because I told him Augie wasn't allowed inside the gates.

"That's a dumb rule," he said, petting Augie's wet nose. "Animals like to look at other animals."

"They also like to bite, scratch, claw, and bark at other animals," I said, thinking of Augie's deep hatred for Helen's precious poodle, Cricket. Taking Claudia's thumb out of her mouth and replacing it with a shredded-wheat biscuit that she promptly spat out all over the front seat, I hustled everyone into the car. Some were happy and some were not; Lee griped because it was hard to drive when the steering wheel was covered with shredded wheat. By the time we reached the zoo, the sun was high in the sky, the temperature was in the high nineties, and the stench from the monkey house was pervasive. "It sure stinks here," John cried out, holding his nose with both hands, "I don't see any animals. Let's go home."

"They're probably inside watching the baseball game," Lee remarked sadly. "Let's go home."

"The animals are only resting," I twittered like the good mommy tour director. "Let's have a snowcone to cool off and give the little animals time to get up from their naps."

"I hate snowcones," Mr. Bad Sport groaned.

"I like them, Daddy," Amy said. "I like grape ones best."

"I like orange," Mary cried.

"I want lime," David shouted.

"I'll take strawberry!" John pushed ahead of Susan and stood by his dad's elbow.

"Get me watermelon, Dad," Susan pushed John back.

"I just want plain ice," Karen ordered primly.

"I'm not paying a dollar thirty-five for a cup of ice. Everyone gets grape or nothing at all," Lee said as he stepped up to face a flustered salesgirl who was shoveling crushed ice as fast as she could.

Snowcones distributed, we wandered for the next

thirty minutes from cage to cage, peering through bars
and seeing nothing but droppings and uneaten lettuce
leaves. As we stood like idiots looking into the vast
empty spaces of a polar bear's pit, Karen pretended to be
near physical collapse from the heat and panted, "Let's
go home."

"There's a giraffe up from his nap." David dashed to
the side of a low-slung fence and we all turned excitedly
to see a slightly mangy giraffe and two guinea hens
strolling toward him. As he hit the side of the fence,
snowcone held high above his head, the giraffe's long
neck flipped down and a black tongue, at least a foot in
length, slurped the entire contents of the snowcone into
its spotted stomach.

"Help!" David screamed. "The damn thing's trying to
eat me." I knew I should've scolded him for swearing but
the sight of that giraffe with grape juice running down
his chin made me laugh, and I was still giggling when I
spotted the small animal barn nearby. "Look!" I pointed.
"There are the baby animals. We can go inside and pet
them." The miniature farmyard was full of signs encouraging the little visitors to touch and feel the animals. It
was the part of the zoo I liked the most and the part Lee
hated because he said he always stepped in something
and had to walk on his toes for the rest of the trip.
Claudia hurried toward a group of tiny goats standing
near the corner of the barn with their heads down. She
hurried right back, screaming, "Daddy, Daddy" as a
small billy roared straight at her, butting her ruffled
bottom and searching her palms for alfalfa pellets.

"I'm here," Lee said, gathering her up in his arms.
She remained there for the next few hours. Perspiration
poured from his head, and her snowcone dripped from
his elbow as Lee tippytoed through the park, his youngest daughter wrapped around him like a fur coat. She
climbed his neck, digging sharp sandals into his breast-

bone, as a proud peacock strutted close by, spreading its feathers.

"The big bird won't hurt you," I comforted. "See how pretty he is," and, clucking like I thought a Madam Peacock might, I rubbed two fingers together and tried to coax the peacock closer so Claudia could get better acquainted with one of God's creatures. She let out a yell that stopped people in their tracks. "I want to go home!" she screeched.

Lee warned me between gritted teeth that people were watching our every move. Taking Claudia's round tummy from his nose and her snowcone from his ear, he too begged to go home. A white-faced David, still in partial shock from nearly being swallowed alive by a giraffe, had talked a sympathetic but tearful Mary out of her snowcone; John was threatening to throw Amy into the litter barrel just for the hell of it; and Karen and Susan were pretending to be tarts to attract the attention of a group of teenaged boys. Lee trudged far behind, stooped and limping, with a weary Claudia riding his head.

Things were definitely turning sour. Out of the corner of my eye I caught some action. "Oh, look, look!" I cried out happily. "Mr. and Mrs. Lion are getting some fresh air." It was a magnificent sight. The two tawny-hued animals prowled gracefully, muscles rippling in the sun, golden manes shaking and great teeth gnashing as if prepared to gobble anything that moved. My quick lecture on the carnivorous habits of lions caused Miss Scaredy-Cat to plaster herself even more solidly against her father's chest. "Don't let the lions eat me, Daddy!"

"For God's sake," he yelled. "Tell her lions eat flowers. I don't think I can take much more of this. Can't we go home?" And he started moving toward a nearby exit, the children not far behind.

At that particular moment Mr. Lion decided to play loose with Mrs. Lion. The fact that she obviously had a headache made no difference at all. Nor did the fact that he had an audience. An appreciative, wide-eyed audience. Thoughts of going home wiped from their minds completely, our children hung on the fence, observing every sensual move in that lion's den. Karen and Susan tittered and the two boys punched each other meaningfully with their fists.

"Is Mr. Lion mad at Mrs. Lion, Mommy?" Amy asked with curious innocence.

"No," I said covering her face with my hands. I was embarrassed out of my mind. "Good grief," I turned to Lee. "What do we do now?"

"Don't ask me," he grinned. "This trip was your idea. You're the tour director." Rubbing aching muscles, he sighed in relief. Claudia had deserted the safety of her father's arms for the first time that afternoon and had joined brothers and sisters to watch the dirty show.

"Let's go home!" I shouted. Not a soul paid one bit of attention to me. I think they would all be there still if the zookeeper hadn't eventually come along with a bucket of cold water.

The trip home was quiet simply because I'd warned each child that if they said one word—asked one funny question—I would have their father stop the car by the side of the road and we would let them out. The only one who said anything was Lee. He said it was the finest Sunday he'd ever had. Even better than baseball, he thought.

He said he bet Mr. Lion felt the same way.

12
The Truth About Family Vacations

ONE DAY HELEN dropped in and, after exclaiming she'd never seen *that* spot on our wall before, she peered at me and said "You look terrible. Why do you look so bad?" I told her we were going on vacation.

"How nice," she laughed, clapping her hands. "I love vacations. They're such a rest from work, study, and the humdrum of daily living. Think how refreshed you'll be after your holiday." Helen thought a trip to the grocery store was thrilling.

"That's a lie, Helen, and you know it," I said, pointing out that being stuck in a car for twenty-one days with seven gloomy children and a husband who seldom consulted a road map could hardly be called festive. We could be gone three years instead of three weeks, for Lee thought that asking anyone for directions demonstrated a definite weakness in character; we often drove in circles for hours on end. "No need to bother people with silly questions," he would say. "If *you* could read a road map, we wouldn't get lost."

Was it my fault I had problems with things like symbols, distances, and being able to tell an interstate from a foot trail? Could I help it if we often ended up on country roads Johnny Appleseed would have shunned?

I always said if he'd just stop and ask someone where

we were, we wouldn't have such problems, and he said he didn't talk to strangers, and I said for God's sake why not? He replied that you never knew when you were going to come up against one who had just escaped from the state pen, and I said if that little old gray-haired lady rocking on her front porch was an escaped con I'd eat my hat, and he said little old gray-haired ladies could fool you sometimes—I should know. I said, well, then, ask a little kid. He said kids were dumb and wouldn't know how to get out of town on a stick, and I said . . . and he said . . . and the children cried in the backseat of the car because Mommy and Daddy were quarreling in the front seat. Therefore, when Lee planned, schemed, contacted an automobile club, made cabin reservations in Tennessee, saved money, and announced that we were going to take a real vacation and be away from home for weeks, I nearly sat down and wrote the auto club a poison-pen letter.

"I can't be gone three weeks," Karen wailed. "I'll miss Sarah Ann's slumber party. It's going to be boy-girl."

"You'll miss it," Lee said with tight lips. "Even if we were going to be home, you'd miss it." Turning to me, he asked what was that crazy Helen thinking of anyway? I shrugged my shoulders and wondered out loud if you dropped the "e" in unforgivable.

"If we leave by Thursday, could we be home by Saturday?" David asked, oiling his baseball glove. "The coach said I might get to play."

"That's only three days." Lee picked up the calendar. "We can't go to Tennessee and back in three days."

"We could make Omaha," I said brightly.

"We're going to Tennessee." He was firm; our family fate was sealed.

"Do they have Dairy Queens in Tennessee?" Mary wanted to know. She'd been spending her entire summer and whole allowance hanging on the stool at a neighborhood ice-cream shop. She was hooked on dip cones and the thought of going three weeks without one was more than she could bear.

"They certainly do," Lee smiled, patting her arm and handing her a dime to reward her for being the only one to show any interest in his vacation plans. Karen was still sulking because she was going to miss her first teenaged rumble; Susan was sulking because Karen was and it looked like fun; David was down in the mouth because he knew that we were messing up his only chance to be discovered by the pro scouts. Amy and Claudia were too young to care what any of us did or where we went. They were like Helen: a trip to the grocery store was an adventure. But deep in my mother's heart I knew what it was like to travel very far with two children under the age of six.

"Can we take Augie?" John asked. "It's a family vacation, and he's part of the family."

"No! Absolutely no!" Lee said strongly. Augie looked very relieved.

"I won't go without Augie." John hung an arm around the dog's shaggy head, squeezing so hard two large tears appeared in the corner of his eyes. "See, he's crying. He wants to go."

"He isn't crying and he isn't going. He'll go to a kennel and sleep in air conditioning, have lots of petting, attention, and good wholesome dog food instead of Kool-Aid and pretzels like he eats here at home."

"Perhaps I could keep Augie company," I volunteered. Hell, I'd even risk distemper shots. "Do they have bears in Tennessee?"

"Probably." Lee looked cross.

"I won't get out of the car."

To cheer me up, Lee promised we could travel through my hometown in southern Illinois. "You'll get to see where your mother was born and raised," he told the children. "And where she went to school and got all A's and where she worked so hard and so long every day as Hall Monitor. Finally we'll meet all of the people she's told us about who were so impressed with her intelligence and ability. We'll see the peach orchards where she slaved from dawn to dusk when she was but a mere babe; the strawberry patches she picked clean single-handedly without a break; the farm where she milked so many cranky cows for her poor old helpless grandfather; the ice house where she carried hundreds of pounds of block ice each day to cool the feeble, hot, spinster lady who lived all alone and was so elderly and pitiful she couldn't look out for herself. Oh, I promise you, we'll see it all."

"Don't go out of your way on my account," I said nervously.

"I wouldn't think of depriving you of a trip back home," Lee grinned. I had married a mean man. But I had to admit he was cute.

Unfortunately for me, when we did reach my hometown, we found the feeble spinster still unmarried but, instead of withering away in a stuffy Victorian parlor as I remembered, she was in a bikini, pitching bricks in her backyard as she prepared to put in her own patio. She offered us straight whiskey, flirted with Lee, and told the children their mother had been a strange little girl who used to hang around her house begging for ice cubes.

That was the beginning of the end of the myths I'd unconsciously created concerning my childhood. So I didn't have total recall. Helen had warned me I couldn't go home again and I should've listened to her.

"Isn't this fun," Lee called out over his shoulder after we'd been traveling for fifteen minutes, and had twenty

days, twenty-three hours and forty-five minutes left of
our happy family vacation.

"I'm hot," Karen complained.

"I'm bored," Susan said.

"I miss Augie," John sighed.

"I wonder if I would've pitched?" David shook his
head sadly.

"I don't see any Dairy Queens, Daddy," Mary pouted.
Amy was sitting on my hipbones and Claudia on my
thigh. Lee was so pleased with all of his arrangements
that I didn't have the heart to grieve out loud, so I stifled small screams of pain and tried working up some
enthusiasm when we finally did reach the small town
where I'd spent my childhood. It was the first visit for
all of them; and because I really was proud of my roots, I
could hardly wait to show off the house where I'd grown
up. "See," I pointed to my home, now grown as old as I
was, with nostalgic wonder. "This is the house where
Mommy was born."

"So?" John yawned from behind his comic book.

"Did you have a Dairy Queen on the corner when
you were a little girl, Mommy?" Mary searched the
neighborhood with eager eyes.

"Why does it look so old?" Susan asked. "Do poor people live there?"

"Somehow I'd imagined a castle," Lee commented
smugly. He looked quite pleased that he hadn't married
a princess after all. But he was wrong. To me that house
was a castle. I remembered its long stairway and the
hours spent sliding down its banister. The pointy iron
fence in front was gone and joyful tenants had painted
the trim a bright pink, but in my eyes the house was
still sturdy, white, and very, very safe. I could smell my
mother's chicken frying in the kitchen, see my dad's
wide grin as the St. Louis Cardinals whipped the Yan-
kees on the radio; feel my oldest sister, Mary Louise, as

she tucked me tenderly into bed; recall childish admiration of popular Audrey's social life as she twirled out the door on a date; and remembered the many hours of fantasy in the paper-doll world with Virginia, who was five years older, and kind enough not to act like an older sister.

But even with my memories, I had to admit that the town didn't seem the same. Why were the streets so narrow . . . the stores so small . . . the sun so hot? I didn't remember sweating when I was young. I took them past the school, and the children dozed while I reminisced about my second-grade teacher. When we went out to my grandfather's farm, the older girls tippy-toed about, complaining of the smell. John and David hung by their heels from the hayloft, scaring me out of my wits until I was reminded by a favorite uncle, who now lived on the home place, that I used to do the same thing. Mary was nearly stepped on by a cow, Amy cried because her dad wouldn't let her steal a barn cat, and Claudia screamed bloody murder because the dirt daubers and flies were nearly as big as she was and bit her before she could bite them.

"I don't like farms, Mommy," she sobbed. I felt as glum as she did, because my uncle had spent the entire time explaining to Lee how I'd been the only one in my family who hadn't worked a lick when she was a girl. Lee was grinning from ear to ear and saying how great it was to visit kinfolk. Ordinarily, you couldn't get him within six miles of a relative. His or mine.

As a youngster and teenager, I'd consumed hundreds of good, strong Southern pork barbecues, oozing with juice and spicy sauce. I wanted so very much to share this taste thrill with my own children; I urged them to order one every time we stopped to eat. They closed their eyes and shuddered as if I'd suggested cyanide laced with catsup. I lapped up the potent sauce, smacked my lips, and tried to hold back the tears that were backed up in my eyes like the Panama Canal. Lord, I'd forgotten how strong that sauce could be. "If you won't eat barbecue," I coughed, "at least try hush puppies and grits."

"Yuck," they said in unison and continued to order hamburgers, French fries, Cokes, and Dairy Queens, missing such local delicacies as fresh catfish, peach cobbler, and pecan pie. And as we turned deeper into the South, the humidity and honeysuckles thickened, as did my accent. "You-all hush now," I scolded John who was tickling Mary into hysterics. "If you-all don't stop, Ah'm goin' smack you in the mo'th." They weren't accustomed to having Scarlett O'Hara bawl them out, so they stopped in pure astonishment.

"Why is Mommy talking funny?" Mary asked. "She sounds like she has something caught in her throat." Lee explained that Mommy was only reverting to her days in the hills and to have patience, I'd be myself again as soon as we returned to Nebraska.

I didn't think that was going to happen for a thousand years.

13

Don't Mess with Dad When He's Eating

THAT SUMMER HAPPENED to be the hottest summer in the history of the South. Or the North, East, and West. I still get sunburned just thinking about it. According to Lee, one of the main purposes of the trip was to steep the children in our country's history. They had other things in mind. The boys, for instance, felt if they learned the secrets of moonshining they could go home and make a fortune in our block alone. Amy watched for Bre'r Rabbit in the bushes beside the road until her head hurt; I kept my eyes open carefully for bears; and Lee stopped at every museum, roadside historical marker, and monument constructed in the Old South. We visited a charming national military battlefield in Mississippi, hoping they would learn something about the War between the States because it was a truly picturesque chronicle right out of their history books. John spent the entire tour of the park hunting for dimes in public telephone booths.

"Look, look!" Lee called. "Here's a genuine Civil War cannon."

"Look, look!" cried John. "Someone's left two nickels in the slot." Totally ignoring the cannon and their father, who was standing in stiff salute beside it, the children rallied around their brother in envious admiration.

He was the real soldier, the true warrior . . . a brave man. Grant's military maneuvers and Beauregard's blood were ignored as their brother collected $1.20 during our tour of the park. He was dubbed Hero as he ravished telephone booths throughout the South. "So much for history," I told Lee.

As we traveled through the glorious and lovely Smoky Mountains, Karen's nose was glued to the pages of a novel about Hawaii. She didn't see one peak. David kept his head in the snack sack, Claudia slept, John counted, recounted, and stroked his ill-gotten money, Susan taught Amy to play Go Fish, and Mary missed foliage and fauna as she searched for Dairy Queens. I looked for bears.

"Did you see something rustling in the bushes?" I gasped, grabbing Lee's arm as we went along a narrow mountain road. "I swear I saw something big and black in there."

"Good Lord," Lee huffed, "we've traveled hundreds of miles, spent about twenty dollars a mile, and you look for bears, she reads, he eats, they play cards, she wants a dip cone. One's asleep and one's like the king in his countinghouse. We should've stayed at home." I knew he really didn't mean that.

"After a good hot meal you won't feel so cross," I promised. Determined not to mention the word *bear* again, I turned my head toward the window so I could admire the scenery. Keeping my eyes closed so I wouldn't see anything I didn't want to see, I occasionally let out a loud "Ahhhhhhhhh!" of admiration so Lee would think he was getting his money's worth.

My mentioning food reminded Lee that the two of us hadn't digested one full meal since the trip started. If it wasn't my wheezing over the barbecues, it was spilled milk or David trying to steal the tips. I'd left nearly every meal half-eaten, and Lee said his stomach felt like an anvil had replaced his appendix.

"It's about time we had dinner in peace," he said firmly. I told him we couldn't leave the children in the car while we ate. "It just isn't done," I said. "Not even if we crack a window."

"They can go inside the restaurant with us," he suggested, "but they don't have to be at the same table. They're old enough to eat alone. When we find a nice place we'll go in, let them sit by themselves, and you and I will eat at our own table."

"But what will people think?" I had to admit it sounded interesting.

"Who cares!"

The children thought it was a terrific idea, and I soothed my conscience by telling myself it would be a valuable lesson in independence for them; that, of course, they were old enough to eat alone and everyone in the restaurant would be strangers and we'd never ever have to see them again for as long as we lived. There was an outside chance that no one but the head-waiter would know we were traveling together. Lee graciously announced that they could order anything they liked, providing it didn't cost more than $3.50, and that they were completely on their own and under no circumstances, except an emergency, were they to acknowledge that we were their parents. "Don't even nod your heads in our direction," he warned. "This is one meal I intend to enjoy in absolute peace and quiet."

I was the first to see the family-type restaurant with a happy little elf dancing in green neon splendor across the roof, spelling out "Lucky Leprechaun." "That's the one!" I shouted, noting a number of fine-looking cars in the parking lot and an outside menu that promised a good selection of hearty dinner entrées. It had a medium aura of graciousness about it and looked just the place for a big family confined to $3.50 a plate. We were ushered to our tables by a confused but polite host. John, David, and Mary (who was nimble enough to cut her own meat) sat in one booth; Karen and Susan, each assigned a small sister, were placed about three stations away. We had chosen a table on the other side of the room; I sat where I could peek out of one corner of my eye at all seven of them. Lee had his back to the whole bunch.

At first things went fairly smoothly. The shocking delight of being completely on their own caused the children to sit quietly and do nothing more serious than blow bubbles in their pop with a straw; I had to try very hard not to jump up and yell no in a motherly way when I saw the waitress bearing down in their direction with a tray full of banana splits and leaky tacos.

"Remember," Lee said, putting a restraining hand on my arm. "That was part of the bargain. They can order anything they want, and we can eat in peace." Turning to his own platter of chops and home fries (which cost over $3.50), he took a deep breath and, with the fork partway to his mouth, contentedly observed that he couldn't remember when he'd enjoyed a meal so much, and wasn't it great to be rid of all that haggling, and hadn't he told me the children could behave if they really wanted to. Wrong! Sounds of giggles and shufflings were starting to drift across the room. The voices sounded familiar. Out of the side of my right eye, I saw a tiny taco shoot through the air as John sought to attract Karen's attention. She stood straight up in her chair, grabbed the back of her neck, and screamed. Claudia spit up her ice cream, and the host hurried over to see if she'd choked on her spoon. Other customers were craning their necks to see what was going on and whispering behind their hands, as the boys, bent double, slapped their knees in mirth. Mary, thinking they were occupied, reached over and busily shoveled their remaining banana splits into her mouth. John, discovering this, leaned across the table, placed menacing hands on her curly head, and threatened her in a voice that could be heard throughout the room.

"Ignore them," Lee said as I started to get up.

"It isn't easy to ignore them," I slammed. "After all, they belong to us!"

"No one else knows that," Lee slammed back and went back to his pork chop.

"Poor Susan has taken Amy to the bathroom sixteen times. I've counted. I don't think she's had time to eat a bite." Nor had I. I'd swallowed two large lumps of cauliflower from my salad about the time the first taco flew across the room and I was still digesting them. Somehow, my stomach told me, that might be all I'd get to eat that evening. And my stomach was right. A full-fledged family fight was beginning to break out in a certain corner of the Lucky Leprechaun. Snappy sayings like, "In a pig's eye you'll tell Dad," drifted over the heads of the eating public. No one had to tell Dad a thing. He could hear it all.

Without warning and with grand poise, Lee laid down his fork, wiped his mouth carefully with his napkin, gently pushed back his chair, stood up quietly, bowed slightly to me to excuse himself, marched across the restaurant floor, and softly thumped seven stunned heads. Diners all over the room rose in unison and applauded as he returned to his seat, sat down, and polished off his chops.

To this day those people still don't know they were *his* kids, and I'm certainly not going to tell.

14

Thank You, Lord. Maybe He'll Listen to Me Now

I DON'T HAVE TO TELL YOU how I feel about spending more than five minutes in the woods. The fact that I was going to stay an entire week in alien (and possibly hostile) Tennessee country without benefit of telephone, television, or Helen made my ears ring and my kidneys act up.

"Where's the bathroom?" I crisscrossed the cabin like a gazelle.

"Out there!" Lee pointed to an expanse of menacing darkness. "Right up that path and on top of the hill." It looked like an awesome trip.

"If I don't make it back, don't let the girls fight over my jewelry," I shouted over my shoulder. Wailing in pain and fear, I dashed out of the door and into God only knew what. The little gray-green outhouse on the hill had weathered beautifully. A rusty lock was its only security, and as I sat there I could feel in my bones the presence of a large number of big bears rumbling through the underbrush with one purpose in mind: to eat me. "Please, God, see that the stench is too great," I prayed softly. My stomach muscles were as tight as a twelve-year-old's. I started taking my scissors with me each time I made the trip, which, unfortunately, was quite often.

"That's a silly damn thing to do," Lee blurted out. "What good will a pair of scissors do you if you should meet a bear? I'm not saying you will, mind you, but tell me what you could accomplish with a pair of sewing scissors against a grizzly?"

"I could ram him in the nose and run," I said. I had great faith in my scissors. I seldom traveled to strange places without them. I told the four oldest children they too could take the scissors, if they promised to carry them with the points down, but warned Mary, Amy, and Claudia not to touch them but to depend on someone older to go along.

Lee had accepted reservations for this cabin sight unseen. He often did things like that. He enjoyed surprises. At first glance, it seemed desolate and completely unsuitable. Chunky branches dipped down over the windows; squirrels peered into the bedroom Lee and I shared with the three younger girls and chattered among themselves as I undressed each morning. Switching a hip at them, I hung towels over the windows and shut out their private peep show. I wanted no acorn-eating animals staring at me in my underwear. Karen, Susan, John, and David shared a small room with two sets of bunk beds, and the girls cried real tears because they had to be in the same space as their brothers; they said they'd rather have squirrels staring at them than John and David. I told them to shut the door when they needed privacy and stick a chair under the knob. The remainder of the cabin was one large room about eighteen feet by two inches, with a slightly sprung and damp davenport, two patched recliners that had long ago lost the inclination to recline, a wooden kitchen table, four chairs, sink, steel cabinet, and a vicious stove. Clean, to be sure, but not a palace.

"Who needs a palace when they can have all this marvelous fresh air?" Lee stood in the doorway, stroking his chest and gulping large gulps of wood smoke from the cabins located sporadically through the trees. It was of some comfort to me to know that we had neighbors who didn't climb trees and that other vacationers had stuck a pin in the map and ended up in the same area.

I guess now that I think about it, it wasn't really that bad. A small lake nearby provided safe swimming, boating, and fishing; town wasn't that far away; and if you didn't count the three hundred miles I walked each day to go to the bathroom, I had more than enough leisure time to be bored out of my mind. After three days in the woods, I wandered about trying to see if maybe Robert Redford or Paul Newman had decided to rough it.

The children underwent abrupt personality changes. Karen, an unusually helpful young lady, became as lazy as a fat hen. She slept until noon, napped from two until four, and then insisted if she didn't get to bed before nine she'd die. Susan changed in the opposite direction. She became the family tidypaws. At home, she picked up her clothes about twice a year (Christmas and birthday) but in the woods, every time I turned around I found her right behind me with a dustpan in her hands.

"Are those girls sick?" Lee asked, running his hand over the stubble appearing above and below his lips. He'd changed too . . . he'd given up shaving.

"No, it's too much oxygen, I think. It's befuddled their minds." This probably explained why John, normally a calm young man, seemed inches away from having a fit and David, the boldest, bravest kid in the fifth grade, sat, white as a sheet, eyes rolled back in his head, if an owl hooted. Fanciful Mary, whose disposition was as soft as vanilla ice cream, turned into a hard-rock miniature crone and screamed at the squirrels, and Amy, normally quite bright, was spending 98 percent of her time dropping rocks, one at a time, down the holes in the outhouse. Claudia was the only one who stayed the same. She still bit anyone who crossed her path and ate only sugar-coated cereals. I floated around in the background wondering who this strange family was. We were all beginning to get sick headaches from so much family joy.

Two days before we were scheduled to leave our little cabin in the Tennessee woods, the sun came up over the trees like a fresh orange, and Lee, sparkling with enthusiasm, suggested a quick swim and a trip into town for supplies. He promised I could spend as much time in the gas-station restroom as I wanted. It was a refreshing day. About six that evening, it began to drizzle. This didn't surprise me because it nearly always rained whenever we vacationed. Drought areas suddenly became waterfalls as soon as we arrived. I'd learned to accept it along with charcoaled Rice Krispies for breakfast and brushing my teeth in public. Lee said not to worry about a storm. He said no one had forecast it. He said this one was probably as far away as Mexico. He was so sure of his predictions that he talked the boys into going down to the lake to fish. And as they sat on a small wooden dock within walking distance of our cabin, the girls and I sat, snug *in* the cabin, safe and dry, giggling over a game of Animal and eating popcorn. Once in a while the light bulb hanging by a string in the middle of the room flickered off and on, casting long shadows over the linoleum, but it wasn't anything we needed to be afraid of, I reassured them. "It won't storm. Daddy said."

"But Mommy, I hear thunder," Amy whined.

"It's far, far away," I said. "In Mexico. And we're in Tennessee." I suggested we all get on our pajamas and surprise Daddy when he came back from fishing. Lee and the boys came in before I finished talking, stamping and clapping Mexican raindrops from heads and hands. "Coming down pretty good," Lee said. "I think we'll have a real thunderstorm before morning."

"Thank you for telling me," I said. "Now I'm scared to death." And, unfortunately, when I was scared I usually had to take a trip to the nearest bathroom and the nearest bathroom was outside, on a hill, and didn't smell all that great.

"You'll get soaked." Lee looked at me as if I'd finally lost my mind.

"Stay or go, I'm going to get soaked," I snarled and, putting on an old jacket, tying a towel around my head, jumping into Lee's breastwaders, and grabbing my scissors, I went out the door.

I could hear the children laughing at the sight of their mother in her giant pair of rubber panties as I fought my way up the path. Lee had been all wrong in his predictions. The storm was certainly not in Mexico. My feet vibrated with electric shocks as bolts of lightning slipped in and out from beneath the cracks in the outhouse. Herded in one corner of the little gray-green building I shivered . . . afraid to go back to the cabin, afraid to stay where I was, and afraid I was going to die in an outdoor toilet with breastwaders around my ankles.

Suddenly a light glimmered in the woods. "Do bears carry flashlights?" I wondered. It was Lee. He was coming to rescue me. "Aren't you ever coming back to the cabin?" he shouted over the thunder.

"Hell, no," I shouted back. "I'm going to stay here the rest of my life because it's so nice. Of course I'm coming back, but I'm afraid."

"It's letting up a little," he cried out. "Come on. I'll help you." He was wrong again. The storm hadn't let up, it had just paused to catch its breath. As I stepped out of the shelter of the building and into the muddy path, Someone Up There in charge of wind and rain put his shoulder to the wheel, gathered together the biggest mass of noise, the brightest streak of electricity, and all the smoke and fire he could muster, molded them into one hunk, and hurled it down around me.

I flew down the path, setting what Lee said later must have been a record for running in breastwaders. It was lovely in the cabin. By some miracle we still had electricity, and it blazed through the inside of the cabin like the brightest sunset. The walls muffled the thunder, and we drew the curtains against the bright lightning. It remained cozy and peaceful while I brewed coffee; everyone, even the little girls, had a sip or two. I was careful about not drinking too much because I didn't want to run the risk of another trip up the hill. The raging world and its miseries seemed a thousand miles away even when the lights went out and we had to resort to candles. When Lee commented on the romantic value of candlelight, I reminded him that three children were sleeping in our room. "Oh," he said, and looked disappointed.

Our beds were comfortable and dry. Finally we put out the candles, kissed sleepy children goodnight, and settled in to finish what was left of a rather terrifying and short night. I'd barely adjusted my pillow for the last time, called out the final "Go to sleep . . . see you in the morning," and blessed our little cabin in the woods for being there when we needed it, when I heard strange voices outside our cabin window. Strange men's voices.

"Do you think anyone is in there?" a voice said, deep, low, and menacing.

"I don't know," said another in a much deeper, much lower, and much more menacing voice. An eerie beam played along the side of the cabin.

"Someone's come to kill and rob us in our sleep," I whimpered, poking Lee in the ribs. He was snoring and evidently hadn't heard a thing. And no one else would hear anything either; I shivered because it was still thundering and the trumpeting of an elephant herd would be lost in such a racket, let alone the screams of a suffering woman. I could hear Helen spreading the news in the neighborhood about the family wiped out in the cabin massacre. MOTHER SLAIN WHILE BEING GOOD SPORT, the headlines were sure to read. "I knew them well," she'd tsk-tsk. "Especially the mother. She never did have any class." Damn Helen. But she'd been right. She told me I shouldn't have come. She told me we'd be safer in a city surrounded by smog and muggers. But we wouldn't listen. And now we were all going to be murdered in Tennessee.

The voices came closer, beating on the sides of the cabin with heavy, homicidal fists. I searched desperately for my scissors but could find only a nail file. It wasn't going to help a whole lot against a bunch of cutthroats. "Who's there?" I called in my deepest masculine guttural tone. It hurt my throat but I thought that was a small price to pay. By now Lee had awakened and was fumbling around in a confined space trying to put on his pants. He was more concerned about preserving his modesty than my life. I was still in my nightgown and couldn't have cared less.

"Where are your scissors?" he whispered.

"I left them in the outhouse," I hissed back, suppressing the urge to shout *"I told you so!"* But I didn't want the last words we might ever exchange to sound harsh; I didn't want to enter eternity with cross words between us. I clung to his back and he told me to straighten up or I'd scare the children. The poor, poor children. They must be terrified.

They weren't. While Lee and I were wrestling in the bedroom discussing my scissors, David had quietly gotten up, answered the door, and invited the strangers inside. They weren't threats to our lives after all, but two nice gentlemen who'd come through the rain to warn us that there was one hell of a cabin fire up the line and we

should evacuate right away. And we did. Fast. Little pa-
jamaed bodies peeled out of that cabin like bullets. The
men stood by in stunned silence at the hornet's nest
they'd stirred up. They weren't prepared for mass rescue. I was the last one to leave the cabin—still dressed
sensually in my nightgown—and before I left I gave one
last sweeping look around and picked out the things I
thought worth saving. I took a feather pillow, talking
Drowsy doll, and a blue canvas tote that contained
deodorant, toothpaste, shaving lotion, and a box of
baggies. I left my purse, watch, the camera, my house-
coat, and Claudia. Lee went back for Claudia. He also
thought he'd just whip up and get my scissors . . . just in
case, he admitted sheepishly.

"Thank you, Lord," I said quietly. "Maybe he'll listen
to me from now on." I knew he wouldn't, but briefly I
had a touch of class. "So there, Helen," I smiled through
the smoke.

The car was the only available shelter, if you didn't
count the outhouse, so we all flocked inside to watch
what would happen next. We were forced to put up the
windows to keep out the rain and the smoke, which was
beginning to roll through the trees in earnest. We were
a sorry bunch indeed, but we were safe.

An empty cabin, only three lots away from ours, was
sizzling in bright orange flames. It couldn't possibly sur-
vive such a stroke of lightning. I knew all along that the
bolt that had driven me down the outhouse path had
had a double whammy attached; and the poor burning
cabin proved it. It was a terrible sight, and our children
solemnly swore they would never, never play with
matches. Smokey the Bear got some raw recruits that
night, believe me. It ran through my mind that I might
stop smoking, but I was much too nervous.

Limp with relief, I heard the sound of the volunteer
fire department wailing over the hills. The children

shouted and clapped their hands in excitement, and John was relaxed enough to slyly comment that Mom sure looked funny sitting in the car in her nightgown. In wide-eyed awe and admiration, we watched as the firefighters battled the fire and put it out. The heavy rain had saved the trees, thus sparing surrounding cabins, including ours. Hatefully, I had mentally tried to guide a spark or two toward the little outhouse on the hill, but they just fell around it, lay on the ground, and sputtered out. Later, of course, I was most thankful it hadn't burned. I offered the grimy, soot-covered firemen coffee and some popcorn, but they thanked me politely and said no. Lee said this didn't surprise him a bit since I was still in my nightgown.

The trip home from Tennessee was spent with a fairly subdued group of children. They almost forgot to quarrel. Of course, John and David related in detail the many acts of heroism they might've come up with if the firemen hadn't beaten them to it; Karen and Susan individually described, down to the last boot, three or four of the young volunteers who'd looked unmarried; Mary worried about the squirrels and how much they'd miss her; Amy sighed because she knew she'd never get by with tossing pebbles in our plumbing at home; and Claudia, bless her, slept most of the time. Lee chuckled now and then when he remembered the sight of his wife running like the wind in a pair of breastwaders and how I'd played hostess in a damp nightie, and I resisted the urge to remind him who'd fetched the scissors from the outhouse.

As far as I was concerned, that showed real class on my part.

15
Never Wear Sandals to a County Fair

WE RETURNED HOME FROM our trip to Tennessee just in time to see busy workmen straddling tall ladders as they erected billboards advertising the fact that the county fair was coming to town. "Drive by fast," I squeaked to Lee, "before the children see we're having a fair." For many years we'd played the game called Do Not Tell Anyone the Fair Is in Town. Rules included turning off radio and television, hiding newspapers, and not allowing anyone to associate with Helen's talkative trio. I even hoped for mass family chicken pox. It would warrant a quarantine but involved no throwing up and could usually be counted on to clear up the minute school started. We hadn't missed a county fair in fifteen years.

"Look, look, Daddy," Amy cried, as we drove sixty blocks out of our way to take Grandma the salt-and-pepper shakers shaped like black bears we'd brought from Tennessee. "There's a ferris wheel. I can see a ferris wheel. Goody, goody, the fair is in town. Can we go?" A dim light shimmered in the distance.

"Oh, Amy," I said seriously, "I don't think that's a ferris wheel. I think that's a star. It's the Milky Way going around in circles." I hoped with all my heart she'd buy my explanation. Of course she didn't, because my children are smarter than that.

"But I hear music, Mommy, and stars don't sing."

"It's the fair, all right," Mary said, her entire body shaking with excitement. "I know it's the fair. We can go, can't we?" The boys let out a whoop and Karen and Susan said as soon as we got to Grandma's they'd borrow her telephone and call friends and ask them to meet them at the sideshow.

"Last year they had a lady who stood on a box and bragged that she had thirty-two children—none of them twins," Susan said. I looked at Lee and he looked at me. "It couldn't happen could it?" he gasped.

It goes without saying that Lee dragged his feet like he had a cement block attached to each toe, but eventually he gave in, and we all dressed up in our country best and went to the fair. Frankly, we had no choice, unless we wanted to live with a house full of grumpy children the rest of our lives. And we saw it all.

We started with the animal barns first. Large white pigs grunted and nuzzled each other, cows bawled and shuffled flies with their tails while blue-ribboned bulls snorted and shuffled the cows; horses stomped and blew whinnies from their noses, and skinny roosters pecked at Claudia as she walked by their cages. Once again Lee found himself acting as a bus for our youngest child. "Someday," he grumbled, "I'm going to go somewhere without someone riding on my head." Claudia, high from her perch on her father's ears, triumphantly squealed and clapped her hands as we passed by a herd of goats quietly chewing goat food and admiring each other's beards. Karen and Susan, itching to get to the sideshow, leaned against the wooden stables, sulking and glancing about to see if any Future Farmers of America boys were about to catch them touring the fair with their parents. I stepped gingerly through the straw and swore never again to wear sandals to a county fair.

We flew through flower, handiwork, and craft exhibits. Well, I didn't; but Lee and the children set records. I darted in and out of farm machinery, patiently explaining to an eager salesman that no, we didn't need a $68,000 tractor no matter what the little blond-haired boy said. Lee stood for a long time gazing at the dozens of canned beans, pears, and pickles, obviously envying those men whose wives "put things up" in quart jars.

"Don't waste your time looking at that stuff," I said, pulling his arm to move him on his way. "I bet it's all sour."

The exhibition building holding the merchants' booths was my favorite. I ran my hands over the bright surface of a beautiful multichorded organ that could do everything but tap dance by merely pushing a button. I watched Lee's face when I told the young man in attendance that of course he could come and visit . . . the very next day if it was convenient. I couldn't play a note but I was willing to learn. Lee pulled me away and said "Let's hurry" and then stood for four hours, in the front row, while a sweet young thing demonstrated exercise equipment; for a minute there I thought, instead of a nice organ, I might be the proud owner of a set of pink barbells. The children spread like molasses and picked up every giveaway in the place, expecting me to carry a conglomeration of free Indian headbands, pencils, yardsticks, balloons, and brochures. "Don't let her touch it, Mom, remember that's mine!" I was instructed as they continued to hand me things. I knew that when they got home the entire collection would go under beds and into dresser drawers and I'd be pitching for six months before it was all cleared out. Mary proudly admitted that she'd signed her Dad up for a free sewing machine, water-softener service, a vacuum cleaner, and two years' supply of feeder pig supplement. "They said they come by the house and tell you if you won, Daddy." She was so pleased with herself I didn't have the heart to tell her that her father often spit on door-to-door salesmen.

The children had bided their time until their parents had all of the silly walking around and looking out of their system. They were geared up for the real meaning of a county fair—the carnival. As far as they were concerned, the evening had finally begun the minute we stepped foot on the busy midway.

Claudia, Amy, and Mary were still small enough to hold our hands and limit themselves to riding the live ponies, miniature cars, and the merry-go-round. They were happy to go around in circles four or five times, waving nonchalantly to us each time they passed us, so we could admire and exclaim how brave they were to take such chances, and as long as Lee and I were there to pick them up when they stepped off, they were content. One quick swipe at a plastic duck floating in water and some cotton candy, and we could fool them into thinking they'd had a decent evening's entertainment.

This didn't work with the other four. Oh, no. They wanted some *real* excitement and stood gawking at the high rides as people of all ages were tossed helter-skelter in the sky, screaming and clutching each other around the neck. They could hardly wait to push their way into the long lines to get their tickets. "Be sure and stay and watch, Mom," they screamed as they climbed aboard to be buckled in. Why in the world would I want to stand and watch children that I'd carefully tucked into bed at night and promised God that I would defend with my life, plummet around in midair.

"They'll all be killed," I told Lee as John, David, Karen, and Susan were carried up, up, up into the sky in a weak-looking box supported by wires as thin as my sewing thread. I shut my eyes and prayed as the box plunged to the ground, stopping short inches above my head.

"Lady, get the hell out of the way if you don't want to get decked," a gruff man at the controls of the hideous machine shouted. Lee grabbed my hand and hauled me back into the crowd of people who had gathered to watch the fat mother have hysterics. I didn't want to embarrass my family but I thought I should be handy to catch any one of them that might fall.

"Go with us, Mom," they begged as they stood in line again, this time for an even bigger and, to me, more dangerous ride. I had no intentions of going with them. I didn't want to be strapped into a seat by a perfect stranger, flipped upside down in midair while hundreds of people stood on the ground below and watched my mouth fly open, my eyes pop out, and my supper come up. "I'll hold on to you," Karen promised. "There's nothing to it if you keep your eyes closed." This was the same sickly daughter who had carried a yellow plastic bucket between her knees as we traveled through Tennessee just in case she got carsick. Lee said not to nag Mom, that he'd go with them, and then spent the next ten minutes standing on his head as his fountain pen, comb, and loose change fell out of his pockets.

"I had to fight three junior-high kids for your money," I told him later. "It wasn't much fun." He had a lopsided grin on his face and said he'd enjoyed hanging upside down like that. "It was quite a thrill," he said. "Why don't you try it at least once?"

"No, thank you," I answered primly. I didn't care if they did call me fraidy-cat all the way home. At least I still had my dignity . . . and my supper.

16
A Happy Birthday
Party for Augie-Doggie

"I CAN'T IMAGINE that you are actually planning a birthday party for a dog!" Lee shook his head in disbelief as the children and I drew up a guest list for Augie's party.

"It could be the social event of the season," I lied. I saw nothing wrong with devoting some time and effort proving to this grand old dog that he was appreciated and loved. What better way than inviting a few of his doggie friends over to share in his happiness at being alive, well, and out of the dog pound. When the county fair closed, there wasn't much else for the children to do besides blow up their plastic wading pool and watch it drain. A party should be a welcome relief.

"Are you coming, Daddy?" Mary asked.

"I don't think so."

"Will you send a present?"

"I don't think so."

"But you *have* to send a present. It's polite."

Lee replied that the day he went to the store to buy a present for a dog was the day they could come and take him away in a butterfly net. Karen agreed with her father. Since she'd become interested in boys, Augie had become a huge, smelly creature instead of the warm, loving family pet. According to her, Augie was a nin-

compoop and if he didn't quit barking at her friends and
snapping at their heels, she might possibly remain unmarried forever. Of course, she felt the same way about
her brothers too, and spent most of her spare time before
the mirror searching for ways to improve her looks and
her chances for marriage. She also baby-sat occasionally
and was saving up to buy a sports car to drive to high
school; because she had about $15,000 to go (at 75¢ an
hour), she had no time to waste on helping with a dog's
birthday party.

Susan, John, and David agreed to be the primary
helpers. Mary and Amy were assigned balloon-blowing
and Claudia would spend the afternoon with Helen.
She'd offered when I told her I was concerned that
Claudia might bite guests that would probably bite back
and with bigger teeth. "I'll take care of her," Helen
promised, "if you'll let Cricket come to the party." Augie
hated Cricket. We all did. She was a spindly-legged,
straight-haired poodle who looked more like a large
black spider than a dog. We could forgive her looks but
she constantly acted as if she had worms and did nothing but chase her tail and poop on the carpet. I said I'd
invite Cricket if she'd have Marilyn Lorraine put her on
a leash and keep her away from the balloons and my
carpet.

Augie's birthday dawned bright and clear. He was
the first one up, and went smelling about the kitchen to
see if anyone had started his cake. I hadn't planned on
cake. I was thinking more along the lines of popcorn and
candy bars. Paw food, if you want to get technical—
something that didn't require licking dishes. I told
Augie he'd have to be satisfied with chocolate cupcakes.
"I'll put candles on them," I pledged. How could I know
the guests would not only eat the cupcakes but the candles, the little paper doilies, and my hand, and that little Cricket would strangle on hers and nearly die right

there on the spot until Marilyn Lorraine picked her up by one leg and shook her until all the paper came up.

"What should we fix to drink?" Susan asked, pencil poised above her planning list.

"Augie likes beer," John said.

"They can drink lemonade or go to the hose for water," I said. I wanted no drunken dogs reeling around in my flower bed. I put Susan in charge of games, and the boys looked disappointed. "She'll have them doing sissy stuff," they complained. I told her to use her imagination but to stay away from anything that required sniffing. While Susan worked on game plans the rest of the children busied themselves preparing the patio. Balloons and crepe-paper streamers flew from every brick and clay pot; Mary had fashioned individual name tags, shaped like bones, to Scotch-tape to the guests' fur heads.

"We won't need chairs," David reasoned. "Everyone can sit on the ground." I suggested he reconsider, since dogs often used the ground for purposes other than sitting. "I'd put up a few chairs," I warned, "just in case." I was happy it hadn't rained. The thought of having a dog party inside our house nearly made my heart stop. It was bad enough when Mary's birthday party had included nothing but little human beings. The living room had been full of third graders, all smelling of glue and Tootsie Pops, and Lee had come home, taken a deep breath, and nearly keeled over. It had taken two days to air out the house. God knows how long it would've taken to get the stink out after a dog party.

For years I'd bragged to everyone how Augie was sometimes smarter than the children, nearly always smarter than I was, and quite often smarter than Lee. On the day of his party he started acting like a real dumbo. He teased the cat, ate two of my nicest plants, terrorized the mailman, and refused to take a bath. "But

you must bathe, Augie," I begged. "It's your birthday."
In answer he rushed between my legs, hurled himself
out the door, and disappeared down the street. "Catch
him," I yelled. "He's the guest of honor!"

Thirty minutes later, two tired boys and a happy,
filthy dog returned to take up their vigil in the backyard
to wait for the first guest to arrive.

My original intention had been to lock up the house
and allow no one to enter until time for refreshments; at
that time, I'd allow one or two of the older children to
help me. But the invitations had included the ul-
timatum that each dog guest be accompanied by a two-
legged master or mistress; and, since no adult would
come, everyone human was under twelve and had to go
to the bathroom at least four or five times during the
party. I had to unlock the back door about three seconds
after the first "Hello, I'm glad you came" and let Marilyn Lorraine go potty. "Don't take Cricket in with you,"
I asked her nicely.

"Mama said I had to keep her with me or you might
feed her bad things and she'll get sick and die." Marilyn
Lorraine crossed her legs and shivered.

"Okay," I yelled as Marilyn Lorraine streaked toward
the house, a bewildered Cricket gripped under one arm.
"But don't let her 'go' on the carpet." Ten minutes later
she was back and Cricket had a victorious smile on her
lips. I knew that I, too, would find a gift package after the
party was over.

Besides Cricket the guest list included:

Amigo: A normal-looking, curly-haired, snow-white
female poodle with an overbite and corrupt morals.

Sable: A magnificent collie with marvelous manners and
brilliant mind, who went completely insane the minute
a storm cloud passed overhead.

Little Bit: One of my favorites and Augie's best friend.

An adorable mutt, Little Bit never missed an opportunity to maul a cat even though most of them were bigger than he was.

Tiger: A rat terrier and the fastest dog in the neighborhood. He looked and acted a lot like Al Capone.

Lady: Our neighborhood royalty. A springer spaniel with pedigree and impeccable background, Lady licked her paws after dining and seldom mixed with others.

Schultzie: A lovable, low-to-the-ground dachshund, famous for hole digging and laying dead moles at your feet.

Dobie: Mixture of labrador and burglar. Very big, born free, and entered any and all doors left ajar. It was not unusual to come into your home and find Dobie sitting in the family room watching television.

Dropping in, uninvited, was Jingle Bells, a fat black cat; she was very snooty because she belonged to a veterinarian's family and ate only the best samples left by pet-food salesmen. Jingle Bells wore a rhinestone collar that was prettier than anything I owned. She sat cautiously outside the guest circle with a "Come near me, brother, and I'll scratch your eyes out" look about her. John wanted to shoo her away but I told him to leave her alone because she wasn't bothering anyone or causing any problems. At that moment.

I'd thought perhaps we'd play a few games, eat and then let Augie open his presents, but, not to be denied, Old Greedy Dog tore open the cards and packages before I had a chance to get things organized. Mary pouted because Augie received better presents than she had at her party and I told her not to act up in front of company.

Augie really did have some fine gifts. Cricket brought a bottle of doggie cologne; there was a juicy bone tied with a red ribbon, a Snoopy water dish, a chit from Amigo promising a night on the town, four boxes of dog chews, a nice address book, a dead mole, several rubber toys, and a pair of brown stockings. I thought of all the thank-you notes that eventually would have to be written, knowing Augie (like Lee, who I sometimes thought married me because I could write) would expect me to do the honors. I tried to think of something pleasant to say about a dead mole and knew it wasn't going to be easy.

So far, everything had gone well. The dogs were behaving and, if you didn't count the marching back and forth to the bathroom, everyone stayed close to the patio. Even Jingle Bells hadn't disturbed anyone. Oh, sure, Little Bit had given her a murderous eye once or twice and acted as if he'd like to gobble her up but he was able to keep his emotions under control. His being on a two-inch leash hadn't hurt. I should've ended the party then—while I was ahead—scrapped the games completely, and let everyone take their refreshments home in a paper sack. But I didn't.

For nearly an hour, we wrestled with the games Susan had planned. They were simple enough—she'd organized a bone hunt, relay games with a big stick, and hopefully would wind up with a trick competition while everyone stood in a circle and watched. And there would be prizes.

The Hunt-the-Bone game was over in a flash when Schultzie quickly buried it in the cucumber patch and then sat, guarding it carefully with bared teeth; he remained there throughout the afternoon, one paw protectively covering the spot. Schultzie's master claimed the prize amidst boos, jeers, and mad barkings. The relay game turned into a "Jump on the Other One's Back" when Dobie, weighing about ninety-eight pounds dripping wet, landed on dopey Cricket, who topped the scale at a simpering three pounds, four ounces. You could hear Marilyn Lorraine squeal for blocks. Cricket, on the other hand, was completely silent. So silent, I rushed to her side to see if she was indeed dead, as Helen had predicted, only to have her rear up and slash open my ring finger with tiny sharp teeth. "Why you little *@#+!" I yelled. The children covered their ears with their hands, and Marilyn Lorraine quickly hauled Cricket to her breast and fled into the house to go to the bathroom.

I turned my attention to Amigo, who was flirting outrageously with anything that had four feet. She'd completely captivated poor Little Bit with her wanton ways and was too dumb to know that Little Bit had recently returned from the doggie hospital and was incapable of doing anything concrete but pant passionately.

Not giving up, Amigo sashayed seductively up to Tiger the Terrier (who had never been inside the door of a doggie hospital), and Tiger, grinning like Errol Flynn, was stopped just in time from embarrassing everyone at the party. I should probably qualify that. Actually, the only ones embarrassed were myself and Lady, who had never behaved that way in her life. The children and the other dogs were completely fascinated and voted Tiger the best trickster at the party. "He gets the prize, all right," David said. Dobie, who had been pointing a Kleenex for fifteen minutes, looked hurt.

All this time, Jingle Bells sat on the fence, her only movement a delicate swishing of her tail and, now and then, a yawn; she was biding her time and waiting for the proper time to join the party. It came when Sable, her collie hair rising in tufts on her back, looked at the sky and spied a tiny white cloud covering the sun for a split second. With a crazed look in her eyes, Sable jumped up, pawed the air, and went straight for Jingle Bells.

"Stop her," I cried. It was too late. Jingle Bells, not to

be cheated out of a free ride, sprang from her perch, landed on Sable's stand-up fur, and the two of them took off, pounding around the yard with everyone in hot pursuit. Everyone, that is, but Schultzie, who remained steadfast at his post amidst the cucumber vines, and Augie, who was trying on his brown stockings.

Have you ever heard a cat laugh out loud? It is an awful sound and one I hope never to hear again. I tossed four boxes of dog chews out into the yard (later to be ground and spit out when Lee mowed the lawn), hoping to calm everyone down, but it was a useless gesture. Amy was sitting on the ground crying hysterically and Amigo, still trying to seduce Little Bit, was pressed close to his side with Tiger at her heels; Marilyn Lorraine held Cricket so tight her little skinny tail was sticking straight out like a broom handle.

As the screaming children, barking dogs, and laughing cat went around and around in our backyard, I knew I had to do something soon before someone got killed. Picking up the garden hose, I aimed it dead center of the whole galloping mess and hoped I wouldn't drown anyone's child in the process. I wasn't in the least bit concerned about dogs and a cat and I wondered who in the hell had thought up a dog's birthday party—then realized it had been my own idea. "Enjoy yourself, Augie," I shouted as I wet myself down thoroughly. "It's your very last one." And, grabbing a nearby lawn rake, I pointed the prongs and demanded that everyone recapture their dog and "Sit!" immediately—right where they were. "Don't move a muscle or a jaw or I'll whang you with the rake." And I meant it. And they knew it. "We'd better do as she says," Marilyn Lorraine trembled. "She's mean when she gets mad."

I swatted Jingle Bells on her cat behind and told her that if she were good, she could stay for the rest of the party. Everyone sat down calmly, dogs lolling with their tongues out, and if you didn't count Sable's nervous shivers everytime a leaf rustled, it could be called a nice party. The most excitement came when Cricket choked on the cupcake.

When Lady left the party, I complimented her on her behavior and her perfect manners. "You really *are* a lady," I told her, stroking her soft head. It was later, when Lady gave birth to a litter of puppies (all looking like little gangsters), that I discovered she wasn't such a good girl after all.

17

We're Not Taking
the Children

"How would you like to take another trip?" Lee came through the door looking like a man who'd found a twenty-dollar bill on the sidewalk.

"Do I have to?" At one time I'd had the feeling that if I could travel, travel, travel every day of the week, drinking in God's wonderful earth with its changing panorama of flatlands and mountains, deserts and oceans, meeting and chatting with people of different backgrounds, I would consider life full indeed. Following our trip to Tennessee, I hated leaving home long enough to cross the street. I felt I could stay safe in my own home until the final drive to the cemetery and my ascent (or descent) into the eternal. "We can't go on another vacation. The children will start school soon."

"We're not taking the children." I almost fainted. We *always* took the children. They hung to me like charms on a bracelet. The thought of going somewhere without them boggled my mind.

"Well, it happened," David cried out, running through the house. "Mom and Dad are leaving." He'd been eavesdropping behind the door.

"I bet they aren't coming back," John said. "I told you not to feed Augie the roast beef Mom had out for supper." And he cuffed David slightly on the back of the head.

"Will we be adopted?" Mary sobbed.

"I don't think anyone will take seven children," Susan said sensibly.

"I know one thing," Karen commented with a cold-hearted gleam in her eye. "I'm going where they have more than one bathroom. And no little boys."

"Grandma's coming," Lee assured them. "And we will be back. Count on it."

"Goody, goody." Amy was thrilled to the tips of her sneakers. "Grandma plays games with us. And we don't have to go to bed early. Did you hear that, Augie?" and she bent to kiss his wet, roast-beefy nose. "Grandma's coming to stay at our house." The dog was enchanted with the idea. He loved Grandma too. Grandma gave him thick portions of honest-to-God homemade gravy and let him dance to the stereo. She didn't toss dried dog food in his dish and tell him to stop clowning around when the music played.

Grandma wore clean aprons and looked happy in the kitchen. She didn't mind sitting for hours over a Monopoly game watching little children cheat. Furthermore, she claimed that when she took care of them our children didn't quarrel, cry, or wet the bed. Grandma was a perfect liar.

When I told Helen I was flying to Boston with Lee, she suggested we make out a will.

"Why?" I asked. "I don't have anything decent to leave anyone. Who'd want a battered bean pot or bent rectal thermometer?"

"You have that nice three-piece suit," she hinted. "If it was taken in several inches it could easily fit someone as small as I am." I hated bursting her greedy bubble but I was wearing that suit. It was the only thing in my closet that wasn't the color of peanut butter. I also had a strong suspicion that if my will had to be probated, the suit wasn't going to be in any better shape than the corpse; but I told Helen that if anything happened to me, the suit was hers. This seemed to satisfy her and she gave me a peck on the cheek. *"Bon voyage,"* she waved. "If Grandma needs any help, tell her to call me." Fat chance. Grandma thought Helen was a real flake. "The last time I was here," Grandma said, "she brought over a casserole dish that had three carrots and a wad of ham that wouldn't feed a bird." Grandma believed in fattening people up. "If you're going to the trouble of heating up the stove, you might as well cook enough to make it worth your while," was her philosophy. There would be no danger of our children starving to death while we were gone. In fact, I doubted they would even miss us.

Grandma was actually smiling when she came up the sidewalk with her overnight bag and a big paper sack. Grandpa didn't look so hot, but he'd had the choice of being left at home alone to fend for himself or joining her at Zooland. "Sorry I can't stay," he apologized, "but there's too much work to be done at home." Grandma smiled, patted his hand, and told him to do as he pleased, knowing full well he'd spend the entire time she was gone moping in front of the television set. "Don't forget to come and eat supper with us," she called out as he left. This seemed to cheer Grandpa up considerably.

When Grandma came to baby-sit she didn't come empty-handed. Along with a supply of fresh aprons she brought along puzzles, sweet pickles, funny old family pictures, interesting stories, hair-raising tales of babies being born in back bedrooms, and a heart full of love for each of our seven children that made them all think they were very special. She didn't talk on the telephone, watch soap operas, or lie down in the middle of the afternoon to take a nap. When someone called, "He's killing me!" she ran to see if he really was. Our children looked so contented and clean after spending a week with Grandma that I often felt like letting Lee take them on a trip and asking Grandma to baby-sit with me.

Lee considered flying to Boston as simple as hopping into our car. I was terrified by the whole idea and did everything wrong. "You're taking far too much luggage, for one thing," he scolded as I packed a third suitcase, tightened the strap on my garment bag, rearranged a semi-huge cosmetic case, stuck a book in a flight pouch, and threw a shopping bag in my purse.

"Why are you taking a shopping bag?" he asked. "Certainly that can't be necessary."

"It will be if I get airsick," I shot back. I'd seen those puny paper bags they stuck into seat pockets on airplanes.

Lee was unusually quiet during our trip. If he talked at all, I didn't hear him. He said it was because I'd jammed my ears so tight with the earphones attached to my seat stereo, I couldn't have heard God Almighty if He'd called down. One of the reasons he'd brought me along, he pointed out, was to have someone friendly to chat with during the flight. "If I'd known you were going to shut your eyes, sag in your seat, and snap your fingers for four or five hours straight I would've invited Ray."

When we landed in Chicago to change planes, we couldn't find anyone to help with our suitcases. Lee had to lug four hundred pounds of luggage on his back from United to TWA. Boy, he talked a lot then. Said some really out-of-the-ordinary things too. I heard every word very clearly. So did a lot of other people. More and more I envied the children, safe and sound back home with Grandma.

Logan Airport in Boston was larger than our entire hometown in Nebraska and twice as active. I was so busy looking and craning my neck that I kept tripping over my own feet. I pointed out an international airline where sophisticated foreign travelers lounged patiently waiting for their flights, smoking long brown cigarettes and looking very mysterious. Lee said they were probably all from Sedalia, Missouri, and that I shouldn't get so worked up about that type of thing. "After all," he said, "they are only people. No different than we are." He wasn't quite as nice about it when I chased a professional football team down the streets of Boston.

"But it was the Pittsburgh Steelers," I crooned. "And I only wanted to say hello and tell them how much I admired their game."

"Telling them you admire their game and asking them to help carry your luggage are two different things," he said, his eyes looking glazed. Well, hell, they weren't carrying anything and big strong fellows like that certainly shouldn't object to carrying a suitcase or two, but I decided I should probably drop the subject. When we reached our hotel, jet lag set in and I implored Lee to send for room service. "I'll have milk toast and hot tea," I swallowed.

"Not on your life. Where's your sense of adventure? I didn't travel two thousand miles to sit in a hotel room and drink tea." Rubbing his hands together, he straightened his tie, asked me please to put on shoes now that we were in the big city, and announced he'd made reservations in the hotel restaurant downstairs.

"But won't it be awfully expensive?" I argued. The restaurant had looked pretty plush to me—unlike our room, which was evidently the afterthought of a drunken architect and about the size of a pea pod. We were paying $89.50 for the privilege of drawing our knees up under our chins when we sat down in a chair, and now Lee was planning to order a full meal in a restaurant that looked like it allowed only kings to sit at its tables.

"Damn the expense!" he said masterfully. I couldn't get my shoes on fast enough. And sweeping into the restaurant on Lee's arm, I felt quite wealthy, worldly, and absolutely childless. Lee looked so handsome in his navy-blue suit, I squeezed his arm the tiniest bit to let him know how proud I was and how much I loved him. We were seated graciously in a candlelit corner and I noticed immediately that the tablecloth and napkins matched. They weren't made out of paper either, by golly. Our waiter's name was Charles and in a marvelous baritone he recommended the "catch of the day."

"I won't eat swordfish!" I leaned toward Lee, holding my napkin in front of my face. I didn't want to hurt Charles's feelings, but I certainly had no intentions of eating swordfish. I didn't care if he sat down on the floor and cried. "Why don't you tell him to have the chef run out and catch a cow."

"This is ocean country and people eat fish," Lee said wisely. "You'll not get a chance like this again." (Who cares, I thought.) "It's a Boston specialty." And he went into a long, detailed boring story about salty fishermen going out in their boats at dawn. "Let me order for you. Trust me." And he told Charles to bring the lady an appetizer of mussels and he'd have the steamed clams. When the plateful of dark gray shells with suspicious creatures tucked inside was placed before me I took one startled look and told Lee to hand me my purse.

"Why?" he asked.

"Because I think I'm going to need my shopping bag."

"Not here, for God's sake," he begged, looking around to see if anyone else was watching. "Try them. That's all I ask." And because he was my husband, the father of my children, and because he seldom asked me to do anything, even sort his socks, I did taste the mussels. As long as I didn't think about what I was eating and kept a napkin over the rest of the shells before me, they weren't too bad.

Lee's steamed clams arrived on a bed of glistening white sand, and he raved to Charles about this original approach. He considered it so clever. I couldn't help but think how violently he'd protested a week or so ago because a good portion of Claudia's sandpile had appeared on the dining-room table in the stew and here he was, paying $6.95 for the very same privilege he'd had at home for free . . . and he was smiling about it. And he wore a bib when he ate his lobster and didn't hit Charles in the eye when he tied it around his neck. I laughed so hard at the sight of my husband in a bib that I took a bite out of the swordfish and didn't even know I'd done it. Wasn't bad either.

"Wait until I tell the children that Daddy wore a bib in public," I giggled.

"Wait until I tell them Mommy ate swordfish with a fork in one hand and a shopping bag in the other," he smiled back, and the two of us laughed our way through the lobster, the swordfish, the sand, bowls of savory clam chowder, and two pieces—each—of Boston cream pie.

"That was surely a meal to remember, wasn't it?" Lee said the next morning, as we brushed stomachs in our tiny room.

"It certainly was," I groaned back. "I remembered it all night." And I had. That swordfish had his snout in my rib cage so many times I hardly slept a wink. I vowed, at that moment, that the next time I traveled to ocean country, I was going the "Whopper" route . . . and I didn't mean whale.

18
Anything That Hurts This Much Has to Be Good for You

IN EARLY SEPTEMBER I read a magazine article that described the upcoming frenzy of the fall months following the leisurely and languid summer. Somehow I couldn't recall *having* a leisurely and languid summer. Most of it had been spent trying to get the four oldest children out of bed in the morning and into bed at night, keeping Mary from beating Marilyn Lorraine's brains out, persuading Amy not to dance naked in the streets, and attempting to break Claudia of biting. She'd reached the point where all she had to do was draw back her upper lip, and family and friends scattered like spilled milk. The article suggested that everyone take the time to relax and smell the smoke of autumn. Helen joined me and the two of us pored over each page of the magazine. She'd brought over her children's outgrown clothes and planned to exchange them for our hand-me-downs. Yet when I tried to palm off one of John's soggy gray T-shirts for Matthew Allen, she took one look, held her nose, and said perhaps I should put it in the rag box. I told her no—I'd give it to David. He'd wear it, I knew. Probably to Sunday school; but I wasn't going to tell her that.

Her children's clothing still had the creases from the box they came in and crinkly tissue stuffed in the sleeves. The clothes had absolutely no personality, much like their little owners, but it was nice of Helen to offer and made her feel philanthropic. It wasn't in my heart to tell her the only ones who wore her castoffs were Augie, the cat, and the life-sized dummy doll named Pootie who lived in the utility room. Helen often asked why she never saw our children in the clothes she brought over, and I always told her they were in the wash.

Helen was bemoaning the fact that Marilyn Lorraine would be entering kindergarten soon and she just knew she'd die without her daughter. I thought of all the days she'd hustled Marilyn Lorraine out of her own door into ours and decided it would be a long and lingering death. "I'll have to find something constructive to do," she sighed, "or I will lose my mind." I mentally ticked off some of the constructive chores I had facing me when the children went back to school and suggested she could start with cleaning out and waxing my kitchen cupboards. "That's not what I had in mind," she said, giving me a very dusty look. "I want something different . . . something that will make my blood tingle, my pulses race . . . something to recharge my batteries."

"There's always old Ray," I chuckled naughtily. "With the kids gone all day . . . ," and I let my voice trail off sensually. Even as I was talking I was trying to imagine old Ray raising anyone's blood past a good tickle. Helen giggled, blushed, and said "Oh, you!" And then she became serious and said possibly there was something in the article we were reading that would brighten our lives. I doubted it but thought there was no harm in looking.

"Here it is," she cried out, slapping the pages of the magazine. "We'll exercise!"

"Not me, baby," I groaned. "I hate to exercise." I remembered the days in college when I was expected to do

150 sit-ups without perspiring. I could still feel the back of the hand of the physical-education instructor as she crept up behind me, forced my head between my legs, and shouted "Do it, Broadway, do it!" Oh that I could, I cried. At my present age and after having seven children, I felt if I did one sit-up my insides would fall around my feet like little anklets.

"It isn't like that anymore," Helen said. "Those days are gone. Now it's aerobics. It's the newest type of exercising that's supposed to be fun. Classes are starting at the Y this very week. I read about it in the paper. I don't know why I didn't think about it sooner. There's no reason why we can't sign up. It will be just the thing, because they are at night and the men can baby-sit and we'll have a whole sixty minutes to get ourselves in shape. You'll like it. I know you will." Collecting a small pair of yellow socks that she thought might possibly fit Marilyn Lorraine in exchange for the tons of clothes she'd dumped on me, Helen went home to make the arrangements for our classes. I yelled at Susan and John and told them Pootie and Augie had a whole new wardrobe for fall, and then went to find Lee so I could complain that Helen was arranging my life again.

"Why do you let her," Lee asked, "if you don't want her to? There's nothing that says you have to let her sign you up for aerobic dancing if you don't want to."

"Impulse," I explained. "Pure impulse!" And the chance to get out at night, I added under my breath. At that point in my life, for two nights out a week I would've joined the Marines. Somehow I had a simmering little sensation that I might regret the day I let Helen sign me up for that class, but I also flirted with visions of myself high-stepping through the exercise sessions wearing a slinky leotard.

"Better forget the leotard, hon," Lee said, not unkindly, "and concentrate on getting into regular clothes.

Both of us have had a long and chubby summer. And too much Boston cream pie," he added. He was right, of course. Since we returned from our trip East I had approximately one and a half outfits to choose from. The rest clung like rubber bands. Helen said I was supposed to wear loose-fitting clothing to our aerobics classes.

"I don't have any," I told her. In all possibility, I continued, had I owned loose-fitting clothing I wouldn't be spending good money and muscles for exercise but would be hiring a baby-sitter and sitting in a smoke-filled room, sipping old-fashioneds and flirting outrageously with my husband. In desperation I settled on a pair of thick, ugly double-knit slacks and a maternity top left over from Claudia; I looked like a middle-aged lady who had made a terrible mistake and was paying for it. Karen grabbed my arm when she saw me in my friendly old hatching jacket, gave her dad a dirty look, and in a heavy tone said, "Please, Mom, tell me it isn't true!" Grandma, who'd come over to keep Lee company while I was gone, was as pleased as punch. She loved babies. Especially our babies. I could almost see the knitting needles clicking in her head as she planned tiny booties and blankets. Lee glanced in my direction and said once again, "I'd definitely forget the leotards," but promised to buy me a warm-up suit if I lasted more than two weeks. That sounded great. I'd been wanting one for years.

When Helen stopped by to pick me up, I noticed she was wearing a skintight outfit that made her look like a maroon pencil. I couldn't imagine how anybody could be that skinny and still be alive. As we drove to the Y, she smothered me with tales about how every sinew, bone, and blood vessel in my body was soon to be reorganized. I had heavy doubts about that.

It was a terrible and dreadful thing to walk into the large gymnasium and find the instructor with her leg stuck straight up in the air and she wasn't even holding on to anything. She was very young, supple, and probably the most gorgeous blonde I'd ever seen. I was glad Lee hadn't insisted on monitoring the class. I didn't think he should see anyone like that. I introduced myself as she stood before me rotating her shapely knee-caps. "I'm Sally," she said, offering her hand and welcoming me to the class.

"Why are you standing like that?" I asked, looking closely to see if I could see signs of sweat. Not a drop.

"I'm loosening up." And she flipped to the floor in one totally graceful movement. She might not sweat but she was sure going to snap a bone or something if she kept that up. "Warming up is the first step in aerobics."

"God, I can't do that," I screamed. "Please, don't make me do that!" Even Helen looked a little overcome.

"You won't have to in the beginning," Sally assured us. "But you'll want to at the end."

"Don't count on it, honey," I mumbled and, turning to Helen, I asked her if she'd try to get my money back. Reminding me of the warm-up suit Lee had promised, she gave me a "Don't give up now" look and helped me over to join the rest of the class. I was leaning on her like a bookend. I looked around the room and saw I was the oldest one in the room. I was also the fattest, the slowest, the stiffest, the only one wearing a maternity smock, and I couldn't find my pulse. "Locate your pulse," Pretty Sally had instructed, "and count while I time you."

I looked and looked and couldn't find it anywhere. I slipped over to Helen, who was standing next to me with a pulse that throbbed like a jungle drum. "Can you help me find mine?" Taking my wrist, she gave me a strange stare and said, "It isn't there. Let me try your throat," and, placing her fingers just above and to the left of my Adam's apple, she shook her head and pressed harder.

"Let me go, Helen," I gagged. "You're choking me to death."

"Well, I can't find a pulse," she threw over her shoulder as she scooted off to do some knee bends, "I told you that you smoked too much." I skipped pulses, deciding anything that hard to find couldn't be important anyway, and rolled my left shoulder to warm up.

"Everyone jog in place." Sally's blond ponytail flipped merrily. I lifted one foot and was immediately cracked in the chin by a bouncing bosom. "Now slap your knees, rock, circle your arms, push out, break, reach, and lunge!" The lunge did it. I was surely dying. Thank God, I panted, only a few minutes left in this torturous hour. We'd soon be done and I could go home. I glanced at the clock. We had fifty-seven minutes to go.

I flapped my arm in the air to get Sally's attention so I could be excused to go to the restroom to sneak a cigarette, and she smiled. I waved both hands in desperation, and she waved back. I extended my body from the waist and double-lifted from the floor and she yelled, "Good job. Keep it up!" I didn't want praise, I wanted my pulse back. I'd never worked so hard in my life.

When the class ended, Helen had to push me to the car. She was bubbling over with health and good cheer. I had no doubt she was going to race home and tackle old Ray to get her batteries charged. I told Lee if he touched me I'd make him go to the utility room and sleep with Pootie. He just laughed and offered to rub my back with liniment.

Three weeks and six hours of classes later, I had definitely lost inches but I could no longer walk up the stairs.

"I think you're getting thinner," Lee said, punching various parts of my body.

"No," I said sadly, "not thinner. It's just shifted. The fat on top has been joggled to the soles of my feet with

all that hopping and skipping. I'm about five inches
taller but not thinner."

"Nevertheless," Lee complimented, "it's working.
You're looking swell." Perhaps in his biased opinion I
was looking swell, but I was paying a large price. The
flush on my face was from blood vessels that hadn't
worked in years; the sparkle in the eyes, from shock; the
luster to my hair, perspiration; and the throaty, husky
voice, a by-product of exhaustion. My pulse, once it got
started, hopped all over my body like a frog. Perhaps I
could touch my toes for the first time since Claudia's
birth, but I couldn't get out of bed in the morning; and
I'd developed a complete and totally new respect for
Augie-Doggie.

"Don't underestimate this dear dog," I told my family, cuddling Augie's shaggy head in my aching arms.
"He's been performing a skill that none of us have appreciated." The dog's eyes snapped in surprise. Was I
talking about his ability to lick laundry soap right from
the box? Did I mean his knack for cornering the cat? His
wizardry at walking on top of the coffee table? The fact
that he looked nice in Helen's clothes? He sat close to
my layered feet and looked up in anticipation as I explained.

"Do you realize how difficult it is to get down on your
hands and knees, hike up your leg, and do an exercise
called 'Dog Hydrant'?" Lee laughed out loud and Augie
rolled over and played dead.

"Could I come watch aerobic dancing, Mom?" John
asked. "It could be the most interesting thing I've ever
done in my life." I told him firmly that he couldn't
watch, and I meant it with all my heart. I had no intentions of entertaining an audience with my poor imitation of Augie lifting his leg to salute a willow tree;
nor did I want them to see me puffing through the
"Chattanooga Choo Choo" or running away from "Rock

Around the Clock." Everyone else in my class, including Helen, seemed quite bright and extremely coordinated. They knew their right foot from their left and didn't keep bumping into the wrestling mats lined up against the wall. Not once did anyone else go into the middle of the circle all alone or find the fetal position personally revolting. While everyone else was lotus I was sunflower, my knee lifts sent sound cracks like pistol shots throughout the entire building, and my cha-cha-cha was definitely dull. In fact, it was hardly recognizable.

"You're not getting the rhythm," Helen lunged at my clumping like a waltzing maroon pencil. "You're supposed to slacken your muscles and boogie to the beat. Swing your arms and let your feet go."

"If I let my feet go," I informed her seriously, "they will go straight home to the refrigerator and a cold beer. My feet are no dummies." Helen boogied off and said she was going to dance with someone who wanted to cooperate.

"Keep reminding yourself how much good this is doing," Pretty Sally sympathized, as she came upon me hiding behind the water fountain. "My goodness," she said, reaching down to tissue my face. "What would you be doing at home that could match this?" So I told her.

"At home," I said, "I'd be reading bedtime stories to my little girls, followed by a piece of peach pie at the kitchen table." Waggling an accusing finger at me, she reminded me that peach pie wouldn't get me anything but fat hips. And she was absolutely right. Aerobic dancing had to be good for you . . . anything that hurt that much had to be. Lee had the bottoms of my warm-up suit waiting for me when I got home that evening from class. He said I had to earn the top. I wondered a little what he had in mind, but, like Scarlett, decided I'd worry about it in the morning. Half a warm-up suit was better than none.

19

It's Always the Year of the Child

IN ABOUT THREE DAYS after the last aerobics class, I regained all my weight, Amy entered first grade, and now there were six children in school with one left over at home. I'd always wanted an "only child" to pamper and pet. True, for a short time Karen had been an only child but, God, all I did then was sit around and cry. Five minutes after she was born I was pregnant with Susan, so I really had two children, even if one was hidden. Claudia was an honest-to-goodness "only child" and would be that way for a few hours each day, not counting holidays and weekends. It was a brand-new experience for both of us. We looked at each other like strangers and kept up a polite front for a day or so. I waited on her hand and foot. She had a lonely look in her eyes at lunchtime when she was at the table and discovered there was no one to slurp soup with. She followed me about the house like a small shadow, and when she took a nap I kept peeking my head in the door to see if she was awake yet.

As I've mentioned many times, we really hadn't planned on having seven children—in fact, we hadn't planned on *one*—and before Claudia was born, we already had what most people considered a pretty good houseful. We'd achieved a nice balance: two girls, two boys, two girls. Add mother and father, and like Noah's Ark we were paired up beautifully. Suddenly, the family seesaw was unbalanced. Disguised as a perfect, dark-haired angel, a jet-propelled force nuzzled her way into our lives, and we faced the problem of finding a place to stash this seventh child . . . and fifth daughter.

"Not in here," the boys yelled, throwing bodies against their bedroom door. "We don't have room for a g-i-r-l!" They'd hardly forgiven me for not providing a brother; now, to add to the insult, here I was trying to sneak a girlchild into their room. I reassured them I would put no babies in the same room with them. "What chance would a newborn have in there anyway?" I explained to Lee. "Dog germs alone would smother her. They weigh more than she does."

"What if she cries?" Karen and Susan bawled. Content with playing mother to dollies who could be quieted instantly by being closed up in a toy box, they wanted no truck with a real, flesh-and-blood infant that couldn't be tossed in a container with the lid down when it became tiresome. In the small room Amy and Mary shared, there was hardly space to hang a picture; another crib would be an impossibility.

"I suppose she can sleep in our room," Lee reluctantly agreed, and helped me shuffle furniture about to make a corner for her bed. He wasn't being a bad daddy, only a tired one, as the 2:00 A.M. feedings no longer thrilled him a whole lot. "It's only temporary," I promised. "As soon as she sleeps through the night we'll find another spot for her." How did I know she would be nearly three before she slept through the night.

Matthew Allen offered to buy Claudia for his mother, hoping a baby in the house would take some of the pressure off him and he wouldn't have to change his underwear so often—and David sold her . . . twice. Once for fifty cents and once for a hamster. Helen was stunned to think I'd prefer a hamster to my very own child. "You are really some kind of mother," she stormed as she carried Claudia across the street for the second time that day.

"Honest, Helen, I knew nothing about it," I swore. "All I know is, I turned my back and David had auctioned her off. Matthew Allen was the highest bidder. Don't worry, I'll get your hamster back." I nearly had to wrest David's arm from its socket to do it but eventually I got the smelly little creature across the street where it belonged and our baby back in her crib where she belonged, and I shook my finger at David, warning him never, never to sell his baby sister again as long as he lived and he looked disappointed and put away his dreams of working his way through Mary and Amy and becoming a millionaire before he was in junior high.

A few years later, when Claudia triumphantly announced that God had come to her Sunday-school class, a visible shiver ran down David's spine and he looked very weak about the knees. He remembered selling her; and a personal visit from the Lord could mean only one thing: he was in deep trouble. When I narrowed the visitor down to the Presbyterian minister, wearing his black robes, David was nearly as happy as I was. I didn't want her ratting on *me* either.

Now that she was the only one at home, Claudia sat close beside me at the kitchen table and helped me compose my shopping list. With this new, one-on-one relationship with her mother, her chances of sneaking such things as jelly beans and colored crayons in as staples was pretty good, and when we went to the store she posed in pink and rode in the shopping cart with a regal air, waving to produce clerks, neighborhood friends, and checkout ladies as she plucked cookies from their cellophane, grapes from their bins, and accepted tidbits of strong cheese and greasy sausages from those people standing around the store handing out samples. "What a darling," a grandmotherly demonstrator said, bending over to tickle her chin and stuff prune whip in her mouth. "I love cute little girls and this one is certainly cute."

"You have a dear child," two matronly aunts exclaimed as we passed by and they slipped her a Fig Newton.

"How lucky you are," a shopper whispered, sharing a package of gum. "She's so charming and well behaved."

Little did they know she had just thrown up in my purse.

Claudia soon discovered that being an only child wasn't all it was cracked up to be. She missed the family lineup almost as much as I did. She was a crime wave of one. Fingerprints on a newly shined bookcase belonged to only one person's fingers; a stolen lick on a frosted cake belonged to only one tongue. If a door slammed, I knew instantly who'd slammed it. A dish dropped on the floor and broken into a hundred pieces held no mystery. Obviously, Only Child had dropped it. "Where are the big kids?" she whined, and took to standing at the door or outside on the curb, if it wasn't raining, to wait for them. More than once I joined her and the two of us waited together.

Amy was usually the first to appear over the hill, with Marilyn Lorraine hanging on to the back of her sweater, and in ten minutes or so Mary followed with her friend Robin, and Claudia was thrilled to death when they played house and she was allowed to be the baby and wear a bonnet. I think she would have put on a hair shirt just as long as she had someone other than me to play with.

On one particular day, however, Mary had left Robin far behind and beat everyone home. She was all atwitter, dipping and swaying throughout the house like a butterfly, turning over sofa cushions, pulling out drawers, peeking into dark closets, and finally when I caught her dragging a kitchen chair around so she could clamber up on top of the refrigerator, I pulled her down and asked her what in the name of heaven was she up to.

"I'm looking for my present," she said.

"You had your birthday," I reminded her. "It was in May. This is September."

"But it's the Year of the Child. Our teacher said. I am your child and I think this is my year." She seemed terribly disappointed when I told her there were no hidden presents no matter how hard she looked, and that I knew nothing about any celebration at our house to observe the Year of the Child. Heavens, at our house, *every* year belonged to them. Why would I go out of my way to pick a particular one? I gave her a graham cracker and a glass of milk and hoped she'd forget the whole thing. She didn't forget. Mary wasn't the type of child to forget something so promising as presents and catering to for an entire year.

"Just think," she said to Susan, who was sitting next to her at the dinner table, "our teacher said little children all over the world were being honored by their parents."

"Why?" practical Susan asked.

"Because they love their little children," and Mary looked directly at her father and her mother. "They give them presents and kiss them every day." Now, I don't really think that's what the teacher was referring to. More than likely, she was trying to explain the school immunization program, but with Mary's imagination she interpreted it to mean presents and kisses. Great murmurs of pleasure traveled around the table as brothers and sisters contemplated love and gifts, with no strings attached. "Sounds keen," John said. "I want a telescope first thing," David put in, "but you don't have to kiss me if you don't want to." Susan wanted a lot of new clothes and Karen wondered if being kissed by Robert would count. Neither Amy nor Claudia entered into the conversation because they thought they had everything they needed, including kisses.

"Do you think we should do something about this?" I asked Lee, worrying that perhaps we'd failed as parents for the 176th time that year. "After all, is she asking for so much?"

"I'm not buying three hundred sixty-five presents for seven children," said Lee, his lower lip stuck out like a footstool. He slapped his hand on the table. "Do you realize that would be two thousand five hundred fifty-five presents in one year? I can handle that many kisses, but if you want groceries we'd better skip the presents."

I agreed there would be no presents and Mary's eyes grew sadder and sadder and David sighed and said he really didn't think he'd get a telescope but thought there wasn't any harm in asking. "But I know what we *can* do," I said, to cheer them up. "We'll do everything you ask for for one day. You won't have any chores, and Dad and I won't nag, yell, or tell you what to wear. As long as you don't do bodily harm to anyone or yourselves, you can do anything you want."

Amy brightened. "Does that mean I can pound on Marilyn Lorraine when she grabs my sweater?" Presents seemed pale in comparison.

"No, you can't," I warned. "Pounding is bodily harm and I said no bodily harm. That definitely means no pounding on Marilyn Lorraine," and I explained that outside of parental interference if things started getting out of hand, they would be completely on their own for twenty-four hours. I didn't count Claudia because she was too young and did what she wanted most of the time anyway, and I told Lee that it ruled out husbands too. "It's not the Year of the Dad," I said.

"It never is," he replied and, shaking his head, warned me I could be making a terrible mistake. I didn't think so because I trusted our children to use good judgment but I began to wonder myself the next morning when David announced he was going to smoke a cigar.

"Before breakfast?" I questioned, but didn't stop him. And he did smoke a cigar and threw up in the utility room and wondered why someone hadn't cautioned him about the evils of smoking and how bad it tasted so early in the morning. I cleaned up after him and didn't say a word. Susan ran to the bathroom to use my expensive creams, shampoos, mascara, lipstick, and eye shadow. No large motherly hand reached from behind the mirror to snatch it away and no motherly big mouth told her she had far too much makeup on as she went out the door. Ten minutes later she was back. "The bus driver laughed at me," she sobbed. "I was embarrassed. Why didn't you tell me I looked like a clown?" I still didn't say a word.

"Do I have to go to school?" Amy wondered. "Can't I stay home with Claudia and play with the Scotch tape?" I didn't say no. I told her all she had to do was ask her teacher. "She won't let me. She'll say I can't," Amy said. "She's not nice like you are, Mommy." Boy, I almost weakened and gave her a present right there on the spot.

I didn't interfere when I saw Karen prance down the stairs wearing my one good velour sweater and dangling over her shoulders were my one nice pair of earrings. I smiled nicely, told her how grown-up she looked, went to the corner of the kitchen, hid my face and stuck my tongue out at the wall, but I didn't tell her to keep her hands out of my things.

"Now's my chance to drive the car," John grinned. He was far too young to drive a car and he knew it. He didn't even have a driver's license; two inches out of the driveway, he came face to face with the local police. He was promptly brought back to our front door and delivered into the arms of his father, who shook hands with the policeman very politely, clenched his teeth, and whispered to John, "I will talk to you about this tomorrow when your mother's silly game is over. You can count on it." John knew right away that he wasn't going to get a present.

Later that day Mary watched television for eight straight hours and had a terrific headache. The cigar boy stayed out past his bedtime. He also had a terrible headache and once again threw up in the utility room but no one asked him why and this time he cleaned it up himself. The two older girls fought so long and so hard without interference, it became boring to them; and Amy was allowed to eat in bed and dumped hot soup on a favorite book, ruining its pages forever, and she cried.

The next day it was over, and everyone was back to normal. Lee said "Thank God," and I think the children were quite relieved. I came to one conclusion: the next time someone declares a special year, I only hope it belongs to me and that I get presents.

20

Pootie Comes to Our House to Live

THAT FALL LEE picked up a dozen unpaid bills from his desk and declared that the only person in our house who wasn't trying to break him up in business was Pootie, the life-sized dummy. "She doesn't eat, go to the dentist, or smoke, and I don't have to buy her clothes. She's the ideal wife," he said. "Hell, she doesn't even talk back."

I remembered the day when he hated Pootie with all his heart. Originally, she was created from cotton and old pantyhose for a PTA Variety Show. She was about five foot three and weighed approximately 8½ pounds. Her arms and legs were jointed and she had plump, mittenlike hands with a fist and two fingers on each. Apparently, whoever sewed her up decided fingers on a dummy were unnecessary and very tiresome to make; they gave her only a thumb and ring finger. She wore a gorgeous fake diamond on her left hand; I supposed this indicated she was engaged. Oh, how I wanted to see her fiancé. Facial features were embroidered with heavy crewel, giving her wide, staring black eyes, a half-moon nose with knotted nostrils, and red lips pursed like fat cherries. Shocking-pink loops of yarn were sewn haphazardly into her skull and stuck out like flower petals all over her head. She wasn't very pretty but she wasn't that bad either. She was the belle of the ball at the Va-

riety Show and onstage danced with a male parent who
was a good sport, her cotton arms firmly pinned to his
coat sleeves, her feet tied with shoestrings about his
wing tips. During rehearsal his wife moaned and complained that he never took *her* dancing like that. "Perhaps if you had pink hair," I said, "he might."

At the end of the PTA performance, votes were cast
to see who the lucky couple would be to provide a permanent home for Pootie. Lee and I were told by a happy
crowd that *we* would be allowed to adopt her.

"I don't want her," Lee said.

"But they gave her to us," I whispered.

"Tell them we don't want her."

"We can't. We won her fair and square. We have to
take her or they'll think we're stuck up." Lee couldn't
understand how our refusal to take home a dummy
would make us snobs. I didn't try to explain, but tucked
Pootie under my arm and sat her in the middle of the
front seat of our car. As we drove home, the three of us,
Pootie was the only one who smiled. I promised, before
taking her into the house, that I would keep her up and
out of the way. I thought she was a little too fast-looking
in her gaudy, rose-colored satin gown, so I bundled her
into my old underwear and one of Helen's hand-me-
down polyester housedresses. I let her keep her diamond
ring for old times' sake, and Pootie became a member of
our household.

The children loved her. She became their surrogate
mother. Claudia snuggled up to her as they sat watching *Sesame Street*. Pootie's soft body was the perfect pillow. She didn't move about restlessly, become bored
with Kermit the Frog, get up, promise to come back
soon, and then forget and go into the kitchen to start
dinner. Pootie was very dependable and stayed put, and
she didn't complain when she was accidentally kicked in
the stomach.

She was dressed in a football helmet and sent sailing across the basement floor like a floppy linebacker when John and David needed another member on their team. She was hung from a make-believe gallows when they craved a sacrificial lamb, scaring their father out of his wits one evening when, looking for his hat, he accidentally popped open the wrong closet door and found Pootie, dangling by her neck, instead. It took two aspirin and the promise of greater moments to come to save Pootie's life that night.

Augie-Doggie circled her suspiciously as she sat quietly resting in the utility-room corner. He snapped at her heels, only to find that if he bit into her she tasted like old socks. I spent hours taking tiny stitches in her flat form until she had had more face lifts than a movie star. She also appeared to have suffered an appendectomy, a heart transplant, shin surgery, and two hemorrhoid operations. Mary and Amy pretended she was the patient when they played doctor; with her multiple repairs, she made a perfect invalid, bordering on the edge of hypochondria. She was splinted, bandaged, and given artificial respiration, and it wasn't unusual to find her happily stretched out on someone's bed with a fever thermometer taped to her cherry lips. She had every contagious disease known to man, survived them all valiantly, and never once threw up.

She went to "school," where Mary thumped her on the head when she didn't learn to read and write. Because Pootie couldn't run home and tattle to mother, the tyrannical Mary was never reprimanded by a shocked school board. Our dummy went through endless hours of scholastic torture without ever getting to go out for recess. I was just grateful she didn't ask for lunch money.

"Why don't you throw that old thing away?" Lee said the day he came home to find that our mother cat had just had another litter of kittens in Pootie's lap. "She's beginning to smell."

"We'll wash her, Dad," Karen and Susan volunteered. "We'll make her smell really good." I told them they should get it done as soon as possible because it was clear that poor Pootie's days were numbered and that she might very well end up head first in the garbage can.

That afternoon Amy brought home eight members of her first-grade class to take a look at Pootie. "Don't mind how she smells," she warned her friends. "She'll have a bath soon," and, turning to me, she proudly said, "They've never seen a real dummy before. We're the only people who have one. Teacher wanted to come real bad but she had a meeting after school." I was most grateful to the committee who'd called the meeting. I served cookies to our little guests and they left before Lee came home, several promising to return later with their parents.

After dinner that same evening, Lee and I were enjoying the early dusky fall twilight outside. It was warm enough to sit without shivering and cool enough for a sweater. In between comments about the lovely harvest moon shining through the trees, we discussed exciting stuff like what should go to the dry cleaners the next day. Partially drugged with moonlight and marital boredom, we were both in a semi-daze when we heard a startling shriek, and the terrorized form of little Marilyn Lorraine streaked across our lawn. She was screaming bloody murder and even after she entered her very own front door across the street we could hear far-off yelps of fear as she galloped through her house, and up and down the stairs. This went on for the longest time. Then I saw Helen slam out of the house and briskly make her way across the pavement. "She's mad," I told Lee. "I can tell by the way her head is wobbling. She always wobbles when she's angry."

"I didn't call the police." Helen stood before me, eyes blazing bright and her head nearly rotating full circle on her neck. "I should have called the police but I didn't."

"Why on earth would you want to call the police?"

"Because Marilyn Lorraine saw a dead body in your backyard. Poor baby is hysterical. Her father is with her now, giving her diet pop and peanuts to calm her down."

"There are no dead bodies in our backyard," I pooh-poohed. "Are there any dead bodies in our backyard that you know of?" I asked, turning to Lee.

"Not that I know of," he said, shrugging his shoulders.

"I'm going to prove that my child doesn't tell fibs," and she insisted we follow her into the back of the house. "See!" she screeched, as we turned the corner. "What is that if it isn't a dead body? My God, what kind of people are you!" And Helen slumped quietly to her knees.

Outlined in the shivering dark was a body, apparently lifeless, suspended from the clothesline by two wooden clothespins. Shocking-pink hair flashed in the moonlight and a diamond ring twinkled, twinkled like a little star. One black eye stared wildly into the night, and, dripping from two fingers and two thumbs was what could have been very, very, very pale blood. It was water and it was Pootie. Lee said he'd suspected it all along but couldn't pass up a chance to scare hell out of Helen and see her make a fool of herself. It took me a while to revive her and convince her that it *was* only a dummy and not real flesh, and that we hadn't taken the ax to anyone and left them hanging in our backyard.

Pootie's bath had come from the garden hose nearby. As she hung, one of her eyes had become unthreaded, leaving her a rather frightening, one-eyed spook. I patted Helen's still shuddering shoulder, a giggling Lee fixed her a strong drink, and we sat for the next two hours watching as she belted down five Scotch-and-waters, one right after the other. By the time she left she was on such good terms with all of us that she went back, shook Pootie's hand, and complimented her on how nice she looked hanging there in the moonlight. "My husband shl'd meet yoush," she staggered.

It took Pootie six days to wring out. Birds sat in her hair during the day and one night a light snow fell and she shimmered for nearly twenty-four hours like a cloth icicle with pink frosting. Karen dragged her inside and sat her near the furnace to finish drying, but a pungent, musty odor filled the house like scorched dog hair, and Lee said he couldn't breathe, so I moved Pootie into the garage until she cleared up a little.

I intended to get out there someday and put in another eye but I never did.

21

You Should Have Seen the One That Got Away

THE WEEK of our anniversary, I wondered, what special thing can you buy for a husband after so many years of marriage? I wished that I could give Lee the gift of a beautiful woman, but what he had was what he got. Perhaps if I'd spent the first years of our marriage immersed in bubble bath instead of baby food, I could've avoided looking like a fat little pork chop in an apron. It's pretty hard to develop nymphlike qualities with one foot in a potty chair.

For some reason, Lee didn't seem to mind; he continued to whistle when I stepped out on the town wearing a serviceable, homemade gray knit dress that was constantly in need of repair. Not once did Lee wistfully wave organdy and ruffles in my direction and expect me to put them on. He was exceptionally kind about not minding being seen in public with me . . . or private either. He patted my cheek and insisted that I looked fine to him and, no, I shouldn't dye my hair blond, because dull brown mixed with white streaks was his favorite color. When I moaned, "But look what's happened to me!" he just asked, "What?"

I wished that I could give him the gift of a rich wife, but I came into marriage owing money for my trousseau and will no doubt depart owing money for my shroud. It was so much easier for me to deal in credit than cash. Somehow $98.50 on paper didn't seem the same as counting it out in actual dollar bills. Not once did he point out that I was an impulse buyer. Well, maybe once. There was no earthly way I could explain to our recently declawed cat (or to Lee) why I'd spent $42 for a scratching tree when I really needed bath towels. It was very ugly and looked terrible in the hallway and frustrated the poor cat so much she took to eating the sponge I had sitting on the kitchen sink. Lee worked very hard for the money I spent so foolishly, and I knew that more than once he'd gone without lunch so I could have a bouquet of long-stemmed roses for my birthday.

True, once in a while, his lips turned white, but most of the time he insisted that money was to be spent. He also continued to stay on very good terms with the loan officer at our bank.

I wished that I could give him the gift of a wise wife, but in all the glowing terms that could be applied to me, *wise* was not among them. I rated high on fertile, but not wise. The corners of our home were alive with the echoes of my shouts and stomps as I tried to make it through each day. Would a wise woman pitch a frying pan out of the back door because lumps appeared in the gravy? Or seriously bruise her foot kicking a dishwasher that had gone on the fritz or plant gladiola bulbs upside down? Patiently, Lee rose to each occasion and took over the job of making meals when he noticed tears on cookbooks; he became an expert at repairing appliances that I'd thrown in the garbage or beaten to death. When the glads didn't come up year after year, he shook his head and blamed it on poor soil conditions. "If I'd wanted a wise woman," he claimed, "I would have married Barbara Walters."

I wished very much that I could give him the gift of an industrious woman, but it wasn't to be. My metabolism wasn't set on dust rag. Even on our honeymoon I didn't make our bed and I saw no reason to change that routine. Oh, I made the bed if we had company, but I also found that shutting a door was a good substitute for shuffling sheets. And I never felt a mop held priority over a baseball game. He had chronic ring-around-the-collar but just scrunched up his neck and wore his hair a little longer and didn't smirk or sass when I sacked out with a good book and cold drink instead of sweeping the floor.

"Good housekeepers are a dime a dozen," he insisted. And I vowed each day that I would change.

I wished each day that I could give him the gift of a patient woman, but someone else got my share. I wanted everything to happen yesterday and was quite cross about it when it didn't. "Surely," he scratched his head in amazement, "you don't expect this child to be born five minutes after conception." I was pregnant with our third child and couldn't wait to see if it was a boy or girl. I waited and waited, and he made the waiting easier by telling me softly there was no other way he would've chosen to spend his life than being the father of my children. I felt I could do no better.

I wished that I could give him the gift of a perfect woman, but it wasn't to happen—not in a million years—and I think he realized it too. I hoped he did because I'd crumpled his fenders, his golf game, his feelings, and his dreams, and I knew I'd do it again and again no matter how hard I tried not to. He sat quietly on the sidelines and picked me up when I fell flat on my face. Most important, not once did he ever say, "I told you so."

I certainly did want to give him a superwife on our anniversary, but I was afraid he'd have to settle for a socket set. It wasn't nearly enough.

"You worry too much," he told me the night before

our anniversary. The two oldest girls were helping me
clear the dishes and I was fretting because I hadn't come
up with anything more exciting than tools as a gift.
"Let's get a baby-sitter and the two of us can spend the
whole day at the lake fishing. It's really all the present I
would want."

"Isn't it too cold? It's October." Even though we'd had
one little snowfall, the sun was still shining hot during
the day, the children were wearing summer clothes with
sweaters, and not one bird in the neighborhood had left
for the South. I knew it wasn't too cold but I wasn't that
keen on fishing. Lee, on the other hand, loved it and
we'd been fishing together for years. In reality, he
fished, while I sat hunched up on the bank bellyaching
and scratching mosquito bites. I seldom wore the proper
clothing and when I did, looked like a bag lady. I felt we
spent far too much money on bait and often pointed out
that we'd invested more in worms, leeches, and minnows than we had in furniture.

"If it's furniture you want, it's furniture you'll get."
Lee smiled happily and bought me a blue canvas fold-up
fishing chair for our anniversary.

"How nice," I said, turning the little chair around in
my hands, trying to figure out what I was going to do
with it. "Just what I've always wanted."

"I'm not through yet. Look at this." Triumphantly he
produced a shiny new rod and reel that to untrained
eyes looked like everyday, ordinary fishing equipment
but to me looked like a polished mahogany dining-room
set. Lee admitted the rusty one with the bent hook that
I'd been using probably wasn't giving me proper results.
"But with this one," he said, "you might even outfish
me!" He laughed in a way that indicated he didn't believe it for a minute. I also knew that if I did, by some
miracle, catch more fish than he did I might as well run
on down to the county courthouse and pick up my di-

vorce papers. Lee took his fishing almost as seriously as
he did fatherhood. As we drove to our destination the
next morning, he talked enthusiastically about spill-
ways, dams, and on-the-rocks.

Dumb me, I thought "on-the-rocks" meant a cool
cocktail lounge and a twist of lemon. To Lee, it meant a
large body of lashing, white-capped water surrounded
by huge slick, treacherous, pointed, hard, honest-to-God
rocks. I should have known that. Although most people
consider Nebraska dry-land country, there are lovely
man-made lakes scattered throughout the state, their
primary purpose storing water for conservation and irri-
gation. Many of them are located in pleasant, low-lying
areas, surrounded by heavy foliage and shade trees. If I
were a fish, I'd live there, I cried out as we whizzed past
a perfectly beautiful flat spot with a pretty picnic table
set up by the calm waters. Lee said it wasn't a good
place at all and picked, instead, an area created by
mountain men and idiots. Horrified, I looked straight
below at the boulders on the brim of the rolling waves.
"You mean I have to climb down there? Why can't I fish
up here?" The car was parked by the side of the road;
even with one wheel hanging over the edge, it still
looked safer than stumbling and standing on my head
down the side.

"You have to be near the water," he said, moving
nimbly as a billy goat, taking with him a tackle box, a
pole, and the bait. I followed with the ice chest, suntan
lotion, three library books, my knitting, my purse, a
small sack lunch, a sweater, a straw hat, and, of course,
my little blue chair. Whistling to keep up spirits and
scare away snakes, I inched my way down the rocks,
skinning knees, elbows, and buttocks as I pushed the ice
chest before me and dragged the chair behind. Thirty
minutes later I arrived at the bottom, completely wrung
out and bruised. Lee had caught two walleye and a

white bass and was breathlessly reeling in what he described as probably the biggest catch in the lake. At the same moment he was babbling about being written up in *Sports Illustrated* as soon as he could get a photographer over, I remembered I'd left all my fishing equipment in the car, grabbed his arm, and shouted, "I forgot my pole."

"The hell with your pole," he yelled back. "I just lost my fish!" Sure enough, he'd done that all right. When I joggled his arm, I also joggled something intricate on the line, and the biggest fish in the whole lake shook loose and swam upstream to spawn or do whatever it is fish do when they're free. "Go get your pole," he groaned as he reeled in an empty line and rebaited.

"I can't." A tear slipped down my cheek. "I'd never make it, not in a million years." As far as I was concerned, I would die and be buried right there under those rocks. Remembering it was our anniversary and that, at one time, there must have been something about me that he loved, Lee scrambled up the hill for my pole, quietly swearing under his breath. All I could do was sit there, listen to his dirty conversation, and watch his pole, hoping Big Fish had told all of his pals to stay away from our side of the lake. Lee hadn't been gone fifteen seconds when his reel went whir-whir and the bobber jumped up and down in the waves. I stood straight up on the rocks, screamed, and waved my arms frantically. A fellow in a sailboat, way off in the east, stood up and waved back, quite surprised, I'm sure, at the sight of a bag lady soliciting from a rock pile. Lee's fishing pole had bent double and the nylon line was disappearing from his reel at about seventy feet a second. "What'll I do?" I yelled helplessly.

"Pick it up, for God's sake, and pull it in," Lee yelled back, pitching head first down the steep cliff. "I'll be there as soon as I can. Hold on and don't let go."

I picked up the pole, held on just as he'd said, and watched his line break. One minute it was a perfectly good fishing line, and the next minute it was gone. Sucked down, I supposed, and swallowed by Big Fish. When Lee skidded to my side, sweating and big-eyed, I explained that it was a rare occurrence that couldn't happen again in a million years. He stood mute, stroking his mutilated fishing gear. I bent down to brush my lips against his cheeks. Snuggling close, I said, "Aren't we having fun, though? Aren't you glad we came? Happy anniversary. I love you." For a split second I thought I might join Big Fish and his pals, but he smiled, gave me my pole, and said I should get busy and fish a little, since that's what we'd come for. I looked longingly toward the sailboat that was now heading quickly toward the opposite shore.

Usually when we're fishing Lee baits my hook, but because he had such a tight look around his mouth and his hands were still shaking, I decided it might be the time for me to learn to do it myself. "What do I do with the minnow?" I asked timidly.

"Put the hook through his mouth or tail," Lee answered.

Oh, Lord, I knew right away I couldn't put a hook through that poor little mouth. The tail seemed more humane. Shutting my eyes, I thrust the sharp point of the hook directly into its wiggling fanny. "I've broken his tailbone," I sobbed. "I see blood. I've killed him." Lee insisted the minnow wasn't dead, only in shock. "And when you cast," he instructed, "cast out that way," and he pointed toward the open sea. With great care I took aim and let go. It was a helluva cast, if I do say so, and went straight for Lee's head, the minnow flapping him in the ear and the sinker landing directly in his left eye. "That way," he said, jumping up and down. "That way."

With a terrific swing I let go of the line again. It

hung in a nearby tree and I spent the next hour untangling my line. The minnow and I were both limp with exhaustion and by now, it was showing signs of dehydration. With every muscle I possessed, I wound up and zipped my line as far into the water as I could. The little minnow's eyes were as round as saucers as he sailed through the air. He'd had an unusually exciting day for a minnow. Plopping into the water, he remained there, pathetically blowing bubbles and trying to appear as unappetizing as possible. At the end of the day I unhooked his throbbing tail, nudged him gently with one finger and let him swim away with his friends. I didn't catch anything edible, but Lee did, so he was in a good mood as we drove home. He seemed to have forgotten that he'd married a complete fool who smelled like fish and was as scratched up as an etching, since he urged me to sit close to him as we headed toward the sunset and home. He didn't smell too great either, so we made a pretty good pair.

"Quite possibly," I smiled tiredly as I snuggled close to his fishy shoulder, "this marriage will last after all."

22
Pigskins and Petticoats

LEE, RAY, HELEN, AND I were eating out. The men had ordered huge T-bones with all the trimmings. I had prime rib, baked potato with sour cream, two dinner rolls smothered with dewy pats of butter, and cole slaw. Helen was hovering over a tiny spinach salad that had three drops of vinegar on it, groaning that she felt like a pig stuffing herself like this. Since school started, our lives had fallen into a routine of humdrum monotony, and "Eating Out without the Children" was filed under parental survival. Ray barely touched his food and had a tired, harassed look. It was obvious that something was bothering him, and Helen was so busy dusting the table and picking the sesame seeds from her salad that she couldn't take the time to tune into her husband. Sympathetically, I touched his arm and asked what was troubling him.

He shrugged. "It's a business problem." Ray was sports and outdoor-life editor for a wire service and furnished news stories, clips, and photos of area sports events. Football season was in full swing; he'd mentioned earlier that he'd been run ragged by the demands of dozens of small high schools in the area wanting coverage of their Friday night games. "I have every available person in our office assigned—even the janitor—but I still have

one town that isn't covered. They're getting nasty about
it and I'm really desperate."

"I'll do it," I said. Ray said he wasn't that desperate
and returned to his T-bone, evidently thinking the subject was closed. Not so. I wasn't going to let such a
chance slip away. I'd always fancied that if given the
opportunity I could've made sports history, daydreamed
of finding myself in the press box, rubbing shoulders
with Howard and Dandy Don, a headset perched on my
perfectly coiffed hair, telephones ringing in the background. This could be the first step toward my big
dream. "I'll do it," I repeated. "Please, Ray, I won't let
you down. Trust me."

"Well, I did promise that someone would show
up. . . ."

"Careful, Ray," Lee said. "You don't know what
you're doing." I gave Lee a dirty look, skipped my second roll, since important people usually weren't fat, and
turned to Ray. "Please. Pretty please," I begged.

"Maybe," he said. I was jubilant. He hadn't said no.
Of course, he hadn't said yes either, and throughout the
rest of the meal I fidgeted like a gnat until we could get
our bill paid and the tip divided. Helen insisted we leave
no more than 10 percent and then quickly snapped up
the rest into her pocket while a surly waitress looked
on, probably planning to mug us in the parking lot.

On the way home, I pinned Ray down. "I really can
do it," I insisted, explaining that I'd had extensive jour-
nalism training in college. Actually, it had amounted to
a three-hour course, and the instructor was, in truth, a
biology professor; after we covered the five W's and
taken two field trips to the hometown newspaper, he
was stumped and let us do anything we wanted, which
was mostly to sit around, smoke Old Golds, and talk
about sex.

"They won't be expecting someone like you," Ray
painfully submitted to my begging.

"Will I get in free?" I asked.

"Oh, God," Ray said. When we got home, he brought over a camera, going to great pains to point out it was very expensive and that I shouldn't drop it, lose the lens cap, or get chewing gum on the clicker. "And remember," he said, "if you want to get a decent action picture, you'll have to be no farther than ten feet away from the players." No problem, I assured him. When he left, I spent the next hour or so practicing ten-feet-away stuff. Lee watched as I laid out a measuring tape, tossed a small object exactly ten feet and then, turning, twirled and professionally clicked an imaginary camera. "I wash my hands of this whole thing," he said and left the room to go to bed. I congratulated myself on a perfect picture every time and fixed cake and milk to celebrate. "If you're good at what you do," I reasoned, "no one cares how fat you are."

I could hardly sleep, I was so excited. And over and over I discarded portions of my wardrobe as unsuitable for such an important job, finally settling on a sturdy brown polyester pantsuit that was discreet, feminine, and wouldn't show dirt if I had to get down on one knee. If Howard showed up, I could always slip into something that made me look less like an overweight mouse and more like a sports personality.

At the breakfast table the next morning, David, who was stunned that I'd even consider such a thing and aghast that his father would allow it, shoveled sugar on his cereal until it looked like a ski slope. Sputtering, he said that I didn't even know the proper terms in football. I explained that I knew enough to get by, and he said that I couldn't find the ball most of the time and that I called the center on the team Fatty. Probably I did; to me, they always looked like a fatty. John, who'd joined us in the kitchen, broke into the conversation.

"If you call them Fatty in public, Mom, you're likely to get busted in the mouth. Real sportscasters call them muscular, solid, rugged, robust, in shape—but, golly, don't call them Fatty." I explained for the fourteenth time that I wasn't doing any talking at this point in my career, only taking pictures on the sidelines.

"Everyone will see you," Karen said, bowing her head. "Nobody I know has a mother who stands on the sidelines of a football game to take pictures. *Their* mothers make relish dishes and cherry pies for the chili feed."

"It could be worse," I said sweetly. "I could try out for cheerleader."

"Well, I'm not going with you." She flounced out the door to tell her best friend Lonna that she was planning to run away as soon as she'd saved up enough money for her sports car. I didn't remember anyone *asking* her to go along. I did invite Lee, though, but told him he'd have to pay his own way. He said wild horses couldn't keep him from going and that he'd believe I was going to go through with it when he saw it with his own eyes.

"Oh, I'm going through with it, all right. Ray's depending on me." I spent the day slashing the air with the imaginary camera, using Claudia as a ten-feet-away model until she tired of Mommy's game and begged for a nap.

After dinner, Karen, Susan, John, and David left with their friends for a local football game, the three little girls went to Grandma's, and Lee and I set out for my assignment, which was in a town twenty or thirty miles away. He was wearing a dark jacket and sunglasses. "Traveling incognito," he laughed.

Football Friday in small-town America is a popular gathering, because usually everyone is related to someone. If they aren't actually on the football team, they're in the marching band, cheerleading squad, pep club, or selling hotdogs in the concession stand. It's like a family reunion and everyone's happy and in high spirits and

competition between teams is taken seriously. I sailed
by the ticket booth, waving my camera and flashing my
fishing license. "Press!" I called out importantly.

"Why did you show them your fishing license?" Lee
took my arm and drew me away from the crowd standing in line waiting to get into the game.

"Because I don't have a press pass. Anybody that is
anybody has a press pass. I want them to know they're
dealing with a professional."

"I don't think it helped," he said as a chorus of stifled
laughter followed us through the gate and up and down
the sidelines. Ignoring cousins, uncles, aunts, brothers,
and sisters, the spectators were watching the fat brown
mouse as she waddled down in front of them, swinging a
camera on one arm and her purse on the other. Lee was
grabbing complete strangers by the hand, pointing at
me and saying "Who? Her? Never saw the woman before
in my life."

It was a beautiful autumn evening. A crisp breeze
proudly spread the American flag in red, white, and
blue splendor as the band played the "Star-Spangled
Banner." As I stood at attention, the camera pressed to
my heart in patriotic salute, I felt a thrill clear to my
bones and murmured a small blessing to Ray for giving
me this chance of a lifetime. The crowd whooped and
clapped following the national anthem, and the two
teams huddled at either end of the field with their
coaches. They seemed like perfect gentlemen . . . so cute
and innocent. I had no idea that they would try and
pound me into the ground before the night was over.
Somehow I'd missed the word *awesome* in describing
football gear. As grade-schoolers, John and David were
allowed only to play tag ball, which required a red scarf
tied about their belt loops and a referee to keep them
from tackling. I didn't realize what it would be like to
stand in the midst of fifty-two teenaged giants, all wav-

ing their arms and shouting, "Get those mothers," while thumping each other on helmets studded with grinning skeletons and patting padded fannies in a most familiar way. A player with shoulders like a hotel and crossbars over his eyes politely excused himself as he put heavy cleats on the inside of my left foot, then he sprinted away, leaving me crippled and in tears.

It wasn't long before I discovered that ten feet away was not the same on the football field as it had been in my living room with a three-year-old daughter. I had the camera poised and ready, but all of the action was seventy-five yards away. I missed a touchdown, two pass interceptions, and several low-flying blocks before I heard Lee's voice behind me. "You can't just stand there," he shouted. "Move around!"

"I can't. I've hurt my foot. Will you hold my purse?" He disappeared and I looked up just in time to greet a football as it landed solidly on my forehead. I sat solidly on the ground.

"Hey, lady, that would have made a hell of a picture," some smart aleck suggested from the bleachers. Off in the distance I saw a pair of sunglasses bobbing frantically up and down in the cheering crowd that was ignoring the football game and watching me make a fool of myself. I wasn't getting too many pictures either. So far, the only shot I'd taken was of the doggy mascot, led on a leash by a pretty pep-club member, as he'd paused quietly to salute the spectators with a marvelous view of his left hind leg poised over a telephone pole.

"Come down here this instant," I shouted into the night air, hoping to bully the two teams within ten-foot range of my camera by using my mother's voice. It worked. The next time I peeped through the camera I didn't see twenty-two players, four officials, and a brown ball at the far end of the field but twenty-two players, four officials, and a brown ball coming directly after me.

Slapping pads roared in my ears and I felt the unusual sensation of being tackled below the waist and hurled to the ground. I lost camera, purse, and dignity all in one swoop.

"What have I done?" an adolescent voice cracked as he stepped back to view the remains scrunched in a brown heap at his feet. "I tackled the wrong person."

"You certainly did, young man," I gasped through throbbing teeth. Willing hands helped me to my feet. Two of them belonged to a white-faced Lee, who announced that he was taking Ray's expensive camera (perched dangerously on the end of the water can), my purse (wrapped about the neck of a surprised official), and his wife (nearly broken in half) home where they belonged.

"Best hit we had all night," the coach congratulated his team, as I limped away.

I told Ray it hadn't been as much fun as I thought it was going to be. "And I suppose you didn't get any pictures," he said rudely.

"Oh, but I did." I proudly showed him a perfectly focused exposure of a dog's left hind leg. He grabbed it, tore it into a million pieces, and shoved it in the nearest wastebasket.

Personally, I thought it might have been a Pulitzer Prize winner.

23

The Shape Is
the Thing

ONE OF THE NICEST THINGS about October is that nearly every woman in the world gets to attend one style show if she so chooses. Spread out like a two-hour banquet are dozens of beautiful clothes. Although most of us know we aren't going to be able to eat at the table, for a little while we can snack to our heart's content. And because our young daughters learned to talk at their mother's knees, their first vocabulary contained words like *Mommy, Daddy, kitty, dolly, night-night,* and *I don't have a thing to wear.*

I used this same excuse as a hint that I might like to attend a fashion show sponsored by our chamber of commerce.

"How can you say you don't have anything to wear?" Lee shook the wrinkles out of his good tie as he removed it from his jewelry box. "I have to keep my shirts under the bed now because there's no room in the closet, and you say you don't have anything to wear. Just look," he said, throwing open the closet door. "There are rows and rows of pantsuits, dresses, blouses, and slacks. I bet there's a billion dollars' worth of clothes in there and you want to go see more. Why don't you have your own style show?"

"They're all out of style and out of date," I told him. "It's all miscellaneous."

"How can you call something that cost sixty-nine dollars miscellaneous?"

"But I really don't have anything to wear," I insisted.

"Why don't you wear the lamp you bought last week? See if the new four-speed blender fits," and he leaned over to kiss me good-bye. As I heard the car leave the driveway, I wondered how I could tell someone who shopped for his good socks in a farm-machinery outlet that I intended to fritter away an entire afternoon observing and perhaps buying a whole new wardrobe. He was sure to go into his lamp-and-blender routine. Or he'd find the blouse that fit fine in the store but funny when I got home. Or the suit that I'd bought on sale that was three sizes too small, but a terrific bargain that would inspire me to lose weight that very day—never mind that it was now four sizes too small.

Maybe I could throw a wifely fit, I thought, and get my way. But I knew it wouldn't work. I'd tried that before, and all he did was hand me a bottle of Maalox and suggest that I lie down with a cold cloth on my head. I spent the entire day planning my strategy. As I straightened Claudia's room, picking up crayons, Tinker Toys, and dead grass, I practiced being Olivia De Havilland before the mirror. When Lee came home that evening, he found me sitting in the big chair in the living room, in the semi-dark, with my hands folded in my lap, my head hanging downward, and large tears settling on my upper lip. I'd sent the children over to Helen's to borrow things so that I could go into my emotional scene without interruption. Not even Olivia could emote with seven children and a dog hanging over her shoulder.

"Why are you crying?" Lee asked, laying his coat quickly over the banister, coming to me, and taking my hand. "Are you sick? Are the children okay?"

"No and yes," I said softly and painfully.

"Did John's teacher call again?"

"That's not the reason." I huddled, picking at my sweatshirt with trembling fingers.

"What then? Why are you so sad? You can tell me."

"I don't want you to be ashamed of me," and I lowered my eyes, looking as drawn and wan as I could.

"My God, what have you done?" he shouted. I had his attention, all right. "What have you done that would make me ashamed of you?"

I could tell he was almost afraid of the answer, mentally running through several things, discounting some because he *knew* I'd never do that, but settling on some because he knew I might.

"I wouldn't want to shame you at the company dinner next week," I said finally, "by wearing that same silly dress I wore to the company's open house last week. I don't want to have people look and say, 'Tsk, tsk, isn't it awful about poor Mr. Lueth? He mustn't be doing well at all. I just saw his wife in that same dress a few days ago.' Nor would I want to shame you by wearing that old blouse that makes me look eight months pregnant, and have friends wag their fingers and talk about us behind our backs. And wouldn't it look bad if we were together and I wore a suit that was too tight and cut off my circulation, and I fainted and fell into the salad bar? Wouldn't that make you feel ashamed?"

He said he thought *weird* would be a better word but had to admit that it would make a bad impression.

"I only want to go look at the new styles. Then I'll come home and copy them real cheap on my sewing machine." He knew that was an awful lie. But, evidently, there was enough pleading in my voice—or the mental image of his wife lying face down in the cole slaw convinced him—that a day out wouldn't hurt. Still, he asked me to please leave the credit cards at home.

The next afternoon, I left Claudia with Helen. I was the lighthearted mama, carefree in high heels and earrings. Oh, I knew I'd revert back to the mama-in-front-of-the-stove-in-bedroom-slippers with sore pinched ears when the day ended but for a few hours I was carefree. The sheer joy of knowing that I wouldn't be faced with dirty dishes or a split lip for an entire afternoon made me giddy.

I joined 250 other ladies in the large auditorium, none of whom looked as if they could afford to be there either. We hadn't worn a bolero since we were six years old or silk since we were brides but, as my seventy-nine-year-old widowed father said when Angie Dickinson crossed the movie screen wearing nothing but a dinner ring and a marvelous hairdo, "It doesn't hurt to look. Not one bit!" He sat back, ate his popcorn, and eyeballed that lady with all of his heart. I felt the same way about the style show.

"This is the year for the tall and terrific," the commentator announced as a six-foot, string-thin model stepped out on the runway in a two-piece suit. All around me the short and squat gasped in astonished awe. "I bet she bumps her head in elevators," I mumbled to myself.

"Corinne knows the pure pleasure of wearing pure wool," purred the commentator.

At a pure price of $75 per inch. I wondered how she held her skirt up; she didn't have hips.

"Winter white is in!" There was a dramatic pause at the microphone so we could admire the virginal vision of lace elegance that appeared from behind the curtain. I ticked off the places that I could wear "winter white." A junior-high soccer game? I didn't think so. Dinner out at a taco palace? Probably not—one squirt of hot sauce and that dress would be ruined forever. If I wanted that particular outfit, I'd have to reconcile myself to sitting in a large box wrapped in tissue paper. At our house, jellybeaned hands would soon whip it from "winter white" to "sticky plaid."

"Here's a jet-black suede jacket exquisitely hand painted in silver for a mere five hundred dollars." I laughed out loud. "Pair it with flannel trousers for one hundred eighty dollars and you can go anywhere."

I turned to the lady sitting next to me and whispered, "What would your husband say if you brought that little number home?" She turned green, fanned her face with her program, excused herself, and left the auditorium.

"Wait until you see the dropped torso," our announcer squealed triumphantly. A dropped torso I could probably handle, I decided, as mine had dropped considerably from so much childbirth, so I scooted up in my seat to see better. A flashing brunette appeared in a reddish-brown taffeta, skintight at the top and flaring alarmingly at the bottom. I would've looked like a rusty Liberty Bell in that dress.

"And don't forget the scarf." The commentator introduced a nice lady who showed us eighty-six ways to wrap, tie, and curl a wisp of silk around the long, magical neck of a very lovely girl. A basic black humdrum dress was startlingly turned into eighty-six beautiful and different outfits. Two elderly ladies in front of me turned to each other with deep respect in their eyes.

"Did you see that, Maude? Hell, I've been wearing those things on my head to feed the chickens."

"Beats all, Emma, what we've been missing. I've got a whole bunch of them scarves just laying around in my dresser drawer at home. I get two or three every Christmas from my daughter-in-law." I could imagine those two dear little old ladies spending their sunset years desperately trying to tie those scarves around their necks, eighty-six different ways.

"The shape is the thing!" Our commentator swayed

dramatically before her captivated audience. "But knits aren't for everyone." About 95 percent of the audience looked as if they were in great pain and the remaining 5 percent looked smug, knowing they could climb into a knit dress with ease. They had burned their bras years ago and could wolf down a carrot salad in six seconds flat. The rest of us lowered our eyes, put our hands in our laps, and patiently waited until that part of the program was over.

"We've saved the best until last," I heard, and thought, Well, we're going to be treated to mink and gold lamé now. I steeled myself, knowing I'd never own or wear either. "Big is *beautiful!*" the announcer burst out, and, with that, the curtains parted. Stepping onto the ramp was a large, rather overweight lady with menopausal sweat on her brow. She wore worsted gabardine with a wrinkle across the rear, and she walked across the stage like her feet hurt. Spontaneous applause broke out in the crowd. I felt like standing on my chair and cheering. Suddenly I could relate, I could identify, I could appreciate . . . I could *buy*!

Unfortunately, I'd left my credit cards at home.

24

How to Feed a Family of Nine on $1.29

THE LAST TIME I SAW a mouse in our house we moved.

No preliminary discussion, no compromise or consultation. I simply packed the silverware, borrowed some boxes from the grocer's, wrapped the good dishes in towels, and left. Lee came home one day in late October and found me scanning the real-estate ads and stuffing corrugated cardboard around the crockpot. "Do you want four bedrooms or five?" I questioned.

"What the hell do you mean by that?"

"We're moving again."

"Moving! We just moved. I fertilized the lawn last month. Let's stay long enough to watch it turn green."

"Well, we can't."

"Why not?"

"*He* found us," I whispered. "*He* is here."

Lee glanced over his shoulder. "Who found us?"

"The m-o-u-s-e," I spelled carefully.

"That spells *mouse*, Mommy," Amy said proudly.

"Hush, darling." I put my hand over her mouth. "*He* will hear you and we don't want the m-o-u-s-e to know we are here."

"Any mouse that is smart enough to check out the entire block and to learn who has the most crumbs on the floor can certainly spell," Lee said dryly. "I don't think you can fool him. How do you know he's here any-way? I haven't seen the usual signs."

"I just know," I snapped. "And sometimes I see swishy things in the night when I get up to check on Claudia."

"Have you told the cat?"

"I told her."

"Then let her do something about it. That's what cats are for. Why do you always come to me?"

"Well, first, you've never had a litter of kittens in a dummy's lap or been hauled off to the veterinarian to have your identity and your claws removed; and, second, I don't believe anyone ever forgets to reline your litter box; and, third, no one cut off your whiskers with the scissors last week. The cat is mad at me. You are not. I don't think I can depend on her."

Lee shook his head and said not to depend on him either. He had better things to do with his time than conduct a mouse hunt, and if I wanted that cat to do its job I could set an example. "When it sees you come un-glued over a little thing like a mouse, what can you ex-pect?"

"I can't read a cat's mind," I said. I had enough trou-ble reading Lee's mind. "Besides, what happened to in-stinct? Aren't cats supposed to have instinct?"

"Don't ask me about cats. I never wanted her in the first place," he reminded me. This, of course, was true. Ill-named Tippy (she should have been Queen Victoria), the cat was a Siamese with a definite pedigree. She reigned over Karen's bed and walked in grandeur with high, lofty steps, nipping at Augie whenever possible and staying as far from the boys' room as she possibly could. We'd fallen heir to her when a friend discovered the market for thirty-dollar kittens was very poor.

"If you think I'm paying thirty dollars for a cat, you

are dead wrong," Lee had announced vehemently. "I wouldn't pay thirty cents for one."

"I think I can get her for fifteen."

"Not on your life. There are three hundred million cats in the world available absolutely free."

"She has a pedigree."

"I don't care if she has two tails and can tap dance. I'm still not paying for a cat."

I traded our friend. I promised to write the scripts for her church's mother-daughter banquets for the next forty-five years and she gave me Tippy. "But you'll have to pay for her shots," she said. I also eventually paid for about twenty-seven offspring and *their* shots, but at the time I was more excited about Tippy's capabilities as a mouser than about her sex life. But she turned out to be a perfectly dopey cat that turned on her paws when the screen door squeaked and beat me to the top of the refrigerator. She was as frightened of mice as I was, and much faster on her feet. But the day came when I decided she was going to have to face up to cat instinct and learn to eat mice meat instead of swiss steak.

"Now look here, Tippy," I said sternly. "It will be cold outside soon and the field mice will be looking for warm homes. I don't want them leasing a hole in our wall. Do you understand?" I dropped to all fours, assuming a crouching position. If I had to teach this cat how to murder mice, so be it. As I squatted by the back door I tried to put myself into the proper mood. "Watch closely, Tippy." I purred as I delicately licked my fingers, shuffled my hips, perked my ears, and wiggled my hair. "You are on a hunt! You are a fighter, a thug, a hatchet cat! You kill and eat mice for a living," I gagged. "It is your destiny. It is the way you pay me back for all the nice things I've done for you. Remember, you don't pay a cent for room and board, you have no utility bills, you don't have to pay for your operations, and I picked up the tab for your shots. I'm going to be writing Mother's Day poems for the next forty-five years because of you. Don't you think you could show your appreciation by catching a mouse?" Tippy arched her back, yawned, and fell asleep on my feet.

I hunched by the back door for an hour, alternating between a meow and a hiss, but not one mouse came by to see what was going on. I put out cheese, and Tippy ate it. I sent out tiny love squeaks, and Ray came from his house and looked around the yard. I tried to skitter across the floor, and caught my heel on a nail, ripping the top layer of skin. Tippy was delighted with my performance.

So was Lee. He laughed and said he thought I should give the whole idea up. "I don't think Tippy is a mouser," he said, helping me to my feet. "I don't think you are either!" The children thought it was a great joke.

"Be a kitty, Mommy," Claudia begged when she became bored with hiding my good earrings in the couch cushions. "Say meow."

Mary laid her head on my lap and said, "That's okay, Little Mommy, I like to pretend too. Sometimes I make believe I'm a very famous circus lady and that I live in another world and everyone claps when I come out in my pink dress and dance on the back of the big white horse."

"Jeez, Mom, I don't see why you get so worked up over a few mice anyway," John frowned. "Matthew Allen has a whole bunch in his basement and his mom doesn't care. She even feeds them."

"And brushes their teeth with Listerine, no doubt," I said. "That's all right, make fun all you want, but you'll be sorry when we have so many mice in this house that *they* sit down at the dinner table instead of you." And as far as I was concerned, that was the end of the conversation . . . and hopefully the end of the mice. But I was wrong.

The very next afternoon, David came from school to find Lee and me discussing the fact that soon there would be no food around for even mice to eat if I didn't watch my grocery money a bit more closely. Thrusting a magazine in my hand, David said that my worries would soon be over. "Dad will never complain about how much you spend for food again. It's all in this magazine the teacher gave me."

I thanked him politely and asked if the article was on budget stretchers or how to feed a family of nine on $1.29? I'd read most of them and found they weren't for me. Helen might get by with sautéed sardine breasts and legumes but I couldn't. And I wouldn't. "I'm always looking for something different to serve for dinner," and I thumbed quickly through the magazine.

"Oh, it's different, all right," David said, leaning over to help me find the right page. "It's all about bugs."

"Bugs? What do bugs have to do with groceries?"

"They *are* the groceries."

"I think I'm going to be sick."

"Didn't you know," David continued, the words tumbling from his mouth in excitement, "insects are supposed to be very high in protein? It doesn't matter if they crawl, walk on four to eight legs, or fly—our teacher says you can eat them, Mom. She says you can eat them raw, boiled, fried, or ground up in little pieces."

"I think I'm going to be sick," I whimpered again. Lee seemed quite interested.

Susan slammed out of the door, shouting, "I'll never eat in this house again," and the three little girls sat quietly on the couch, mouths open in surprise. They all three remembered having their teeth cleaned thoroughly with scouring powder after eating something as bland as mudpies, and now a revered older brother—*and* his teacher—recommended eating bugs. Karen mumbled something about having invited a new boyfriend over for Sunday dinner but that she guessed she'd call and cancel that. Augie was bored with the whole conversation. Heavens, he'd dined on Dog Chow laced with crickets for years; bug-eating was no big deal.

John was the only one who showed absolutely no reaction at all because he was curled up on the couch reading an adolescent sex manual handed out by his hygiene teacher. To judge by the look in his round eyes, food was not high on his priority list at this particular time. Possibly he was discovering appetites that might prove more tiresome to his parents than bug-eating.

Finding himself the center of attention, David warmed up to his subject and continued eagerly. "Just think, Mom, no more standing in line at the supermarket. All you have to do to prepare meals is run outside in the backyard with a quart jar!"

"*Voilà!* Instant bugburgers," Lee cried.

I quietly thrust my eyes upward and whispered, "Get me through this and I'll never complain about the price of meat again. I promise!" And glancing over at John, who was licking his lips, I added that we might want to discuss a few other matters later, however.

"You're looking at this all wrong," David said seriously. "You eat pigs and cows. Just think of them as big bugs."

"I have yet to see a cow sitting on our windowsill or a pig slinking under the sink."

"And we can catch them for you and you can cook them," David suggested.

"Terrific!"

"And you can bake them, stew them, or put them in pizza—and Teacher said all you need to do is add salt, pepper, and a bit of parsley and they're all dressed up and good enough for company."

"Not *my* company," Karen sneered.

"And it's cheap, Mom," David added. "You've got to admit it's cheap." He certainly had me there.

"What does it say about moths?" Lee asked. "Could we eat moths? We had enough in our mailbox this summer to feed the whole neighborhood for a year. If we could freeze them we wouldn't have to buy anything but bread and milk for a long, long time."

"I think I'm going to be sick."

David thought it over carefully and said he felt we probably could eat moths. "The magazine doesn't mention them but it says we can eat butterflies."

Mary began to cry.

"But you have to be careful with honeybees. They bite back."

"Good for them," I cheered.

"And forget about striped caterpillars. You can't eat them. Sour. You can't eat fuzzy worms either."

I told him that I wouldn't.

"And you don't want dead bugs because when they're alive, the juices are better."

"Now I know I'm going to be sick," I wailed.

"Can you barbecue bees?" Lee grinned, looking in my direction. "You always like it when I barbecue."

"I suppose you could if you wrapped them in foil first. I think when they felt the heat they'd fly away," David reasoned.

Somehow the thought of eighty-two bees with butter-basted backs, buzzing about the block, made me giggle and I decided to dismiss the whole thing as one of ten-year-old David's pipedreams. I'd just let his wife cook bugs for him someday—though I would never go to their house to eat.

Changing the subject, I suggested to David that we

could discuss his upcoming birthday and who he might want to invite and what he might want served. He said that he had at least twenty-three close friends who should be invited and that if I could get the University of Nebraska football team and their coaches to come, he'd like that a lot. As for lunch, "T-bones and French fries would be good"; he smacked his lips.

"Oh, I don't know," I smiled secretly. "I have something else in mind."

"What?" he asked.

"Just something."

"Tell me, Mom, please tell me." He turned on a charming David-smile. The same one that gave him B-pluses in math instead of C-minuses.

"I think I'll serve a glass of water and a spoonful of spiders to everyone," I smiled. As far as I'm concerned, you don't fool around with Mother Nature . . . or Mother Lueth.

25

Dead Heads Don't Smoke

I HELD THE DOOR OPEN and smiled gently as the entire fifth grade of Starr School trooped into the house. It was David's birthday party, and, much against my better judgment, he'd invited *everyone*.

"I didn't know who to leave out!" he'd whined.

"I know," John said. "The girls."

"But I like girls." And David *did* like girls. Since the age of six, he'd handed out engagement presents to any little girl who happened to pass in front of his desk. The presents ranged from a miniature plastic Sunday-school picture of Jesus to the only dinner ring I'd ever owned, so it was no surprise to me to discover he'd included girls on his invitation list—though I'd told him there would definitely be no kissing games.

"Let's make it a combination Halloween–birthday party and let everyone come in costume," I suggested. "And we'll bob for apples and play Pin the Sheet on the Spook."

"That sounds dumb, Mom. I'd rather have a séance."

"Where in the world did you ever hear of a séance?" I asked him. "Séances border on witchcraft. I won't have that sort of thing in my house."

"Our teacher told us people do it all the time. She said they sit around this big table, hold hands, and moan; then ghosts talk to you and tell tales about

188

heaven and ask questions like, 'Who spent all the insurance money?' and sometimes some of the people faint or throw up because they're the ones who spent it. It sounds like more fun than bobbing for apples."

He was absolutely right about that; but I wanted no fainting or throwing up on the rug if I could possibly avoid it, and told him there would be no séance.

"Can't we do *something* scary?" he pleaded. "The party will be a bust if it isn't scary." Suddenly his eyes turned watery and I weakened, as mothers often do, and I said I'd think about it and went in to study my cookbook to find a recipe for a birthday cake that would feed twenty-three fifth graders . . . with seconds.

His birthday came on the heels of a fall rainstorm. The trees had lost their last summer leaves and stood naked against the gray October sky. They looked Halloweeny indeed; if you squinted your eyes just right, you could almost see the outline of mythical beings in black hats sitting on the branches playing gin rummy. Leftover chilly raindrops lackadaisically plop-plopped on the sidewalk, and I kept running back and forth to the outdoor thermometer, checking the temperature, hoping against hope that it would suddenly rise to a whopping 98.6 degrees instead of hovering just a twit above the freezing mark.

"They can't play outside if it's damp and cold," I wailed to Lee. "They'll be inside for a full ninety minutes. What will I do with them for ninety minutes? David's expecting something spectacular—and all I have, so far, is a bucket of water, a few wormy apples, and an old sheet."

"Don't you have a cake?"

Oh yes, I had a cake. A very large cake. I'd combined my mother's recipe for devil's-food cake with a spicy gingerbread concoction ripped from a woman's magazine, and had ended up with a "devilbread" so heavy I could hardly lift it from the oven. It would be just about right

for twenty-three kids. I had decorated it in bright orange frosting; greenish-black jack-o'-lanterns leered
biliously, but jovially, from its surface. David said no
one would eat it, but I thought they might. In fact, I'd
planned on it, setting aside twenty minutes of party
time for digesting cake. This left me with only seventy
minutes to fill.

Three hours before the party was due to start, I was
pacing nervously up and down, blowing up an occasional
balloon, counting napkins, and peeking into the kitchen
every so often to see if the cake was still intact. Ordinarily, a freshly baked cake, standing unprotected, was
an open invitation to finger jabs and uninvited bites.
But everyone was giving this cake a wide path. Claudia
fearfully cried that the cake was going to hop off the
table and eat *her*.

I'd collected a few quart jars, still smelling strongly
of pickle juice, and a dozen clothespins, but knew that
"Dropping Clothespins in a Stinking Jar" would last
about 30 seconds—including handing out prizes. I still
had 69½ minutes to come up with something scary.

With a marvelous inspirational flash, I remembered
an apparatus left over from my college days, stacked
away in the garage for a day that I might need it. This
was definitely the day. It was a contraption worn for a
Beaux Arts ball; a hinged wooden square that had
slipped over my head and around my neck, enabling me
to drape quantities of gauze material over my shoulders,
hitch on wings, and go to the ball as a beautiful and
slightly tipsy fairy butterfly. I knew there was no way I
could work a fairy butterfly into the scheme of a scary
Halloween party; but the slip-over-the-head apparatus
was exactly what I needed to implement a brilliant idea.
Now all I had to do was persuade Lee to go along with
the act. It would be a real surprise for David's guests. I
was sure of that.

"You do want to make this party a success, don't

you?" I asked Lee, pressing a tiny kiss into the palm of his hand.

He looked quite amazed at my midday passion and said, doubtfully, "I suppose. It depends on what I have to do."

"Trust me!" And because I had the right idea and the right husband, it didn't take long for me to put my imagination to work. "This is going to be just the thing," I chuckled with pure delight as I smeared green grease-paint generously over Lee's face, adding a mixture of purple, red, and gray to emphasize ghoulish eyes.

"Dad looks dead," Susan observed.

"That's how I want him to look." And I used both thumbs to mark out awful hollows beneath his eyes.

"If you continue to gouge my eyeballs like that," Lee complained, "I may very well be honestly blind along with being seemingly dead. What *are* you doing, any-way?"

"You'll see. The children will be here in a few min-utes. I have to hurry. I don't have time to explain." Dragging two card tables into the middle of the living room, I slipped a hassock between them, asked Lee to sit on it, rested the hinged square on his shoulders, shoved the tables together and dramatically draped sheets around his neck, making sure they fell to the floor, hid-ing the grown-up body that was hunched up on the hassock. This happened so fast, Lee had no time to fur-ther question his wife's peculiar behavior. When I stepped back to admire my handiwork, the expression of pure woe on his face made him look for all the world like a dead head resting on a long table. I clapped my hands happily. For a final effect I placed a blood-red-catsup–covered knife in a prominent place near his chin, turned the lights on very, very low, and waited for our first guest to arrive. When the doorbell rang, an-nouncing the beginning of the party, I patted Lee's cheek and said, "Do your stuff, honey!" A tremendous moan filled the room.

"Perfect! You'll scare the little buggers to death."

"I have a cramp in my left leg," he cried.

"It will go away, I promise," and I stepped to the door to smile gently as the fifth graders arrived. Most of the boys had put on their dads' old fishing clothes and were dressed as bums; the majority of the girls were cheerleaders, and one had come as a bride. Matthew Allen had come as a cheerleader, too, in one of Helen's old high-school spirit suits, which led to many snickers and jeers from John and David. The two older girls had left the house, swearing they wanted nothing to do with such a party. Mary and Amy stood wide-eyed and mesmerized by the sight of their father's head as a centerpiece. Claudia had been put to bed because she was limp with fear of the cake; and Augie was sniffing about the card tables much the same way he sniffed around the neighborhood cats before attacking. Poor Lee looked more and more terrorized and more—and more the way I'd hoped he would look. In the soft darkness, he really *did* look horribly dead.

"It's dark in here!" someone cried as twenty-three jostling partygoers thrust presents at David and milled about in the front foyer. "Aren't we going to get to come inside the house?"

"This is some party," another snorted. "I think I'll go home," the little bride sniffled.

"If each of you will wait your turn," I said, "I have a surprise." Leading them up the stairway and introducing them one at a time to the Head should take about 30 minutes. This left me only 39½ before cake.

I took the crying bride first. One swift look at Lee and she let out such a scream, the other twenty-two were paralyzed into complete quiet. She sat, trancelike, on the couch as the others followed. Each reacted differently and each was as subdued as cotton. This was certainly working out well, I thought, and Lee was doing great. I did have to tweak his left ear once, however, when Matthew Allen, pom-poms quivering, stood before him.

"You're grinning," I whispered. "You can't grin."

"Can I have a cigarette?"

"Dead heads don't smoke."

"Do they go to the bathroom?"

"Not until the party's over." I announced that now we would drop clothespins in a quart jar for 39½ minutes. A couple of the boys mocked this in loud voices, but a low keening from the vicinity of the card tables snapped them to attention and they volunteered to go first . . . missing 10 out of the 12 drops. The sad little bride trembled as though she were approaching the nuptial bed and couldn't even close her fingers to grasp the clothespins, so I told her she didn't have to compete. John won first prize because he wasn't in the least bit scared, and David was opening his presents in the kitchen. Everything was in perfect control right up until I served the cake and Matthew Allen blew my cover.

"I won't eat this," he said, pushing the "devilbread" away. "It looks like poison."

"Eat it . . . or I might feed you to the Head . . . pom-poms and all," I hissed.

"I don't think it's a real head," he said.

"And just what might it be, Mr. Know-It-All?" The kid was getting more and more like his mother every day.

"I think it's Mr. Lueth."

"I think it's Mr. Lueth, too," another said. And another. And another.

"I think it's a dead head," Little Bride quaked. She was turning out to be my very favorite fifth grader. I considered her a suitable choice as perhaps a really truly bride for David someday when they both grew up. But he said, Heck, no, she'd brought him a toothbrush in a holder shaped like a toadstool as a birthday present. He said he was going to propose to the slightly wicked girl who'd wrapped a package of chewing tobacco and a baseball, and promised to meet him in the tree house after school.

"It *is* Mr. Lueth." Matthew Allen stepped smartly over to the table, looking directly in Lee's face. "You're not dead, are you? I saw your eyelids move."

"Can I get up now," Lee asked. "I really *do* have to go to the bathroom!" Rising up from the hassock, he pushed aside the card tables and emerged with the white sheets falling from his shoulders in ghostly folds. One look and the little bride, her eyes rolling back in her head like ball bearings, sank to the floor.

"Is she all right?" Lee stooped down beside her. "Are you all right?"

"I'm a good girl," the little bride murmured. "Please don't let it get me."

"You're safe, honey," I said as I picked her up from the floor and held her quietly on my lap. "We'll call your mother right now, and have her come and take you home. I'll send along some cake." Her mother took one look at the disheveled, pale child-bride and surely suspected she'd been robbed of her virginity at a fifth-grade birthday party. She snorted, "What went on at this party, for goodness' sake?" and carried her daughter off before I could even give her the cake. Perhaps this was just as well, because I had fourteen calls that night and the next day, asking what in the world their children had eaten at David's party that had caused such nightmares and the trots.

Helen, bless her, came over and asked for the recipe for my "devilbread." She said Matthew Allen had had a wonderful time at the party. Isn't it nice how you can always count on a good friend?

26

The Popsicle Man Doesn't Come in November

"WHERE ARE YOU, MOM?" Susan cried out as she entered the house.

"Under here," I said weakly from the living-room couch. Pushing aside three blankets, a heating pad, and two thousand used Kleenex, I gazed through a mist of germs to see her scoop Claudia up from the floor, where she was happily splashing in the melted November snow left by Amy's snow boots. Completely ignoring the fact that I was probably dying, Susan pressed on. "It's cold outside. Why is the baby licking dirty snow? What's for supper?"

"It's cold because it's winter. It keeps her quiet. We're having cough medicine for supper."

"Ugh! I'm not eating." She stood over me, a muddy-faced Claudia at her side. "Are you sick?"

"No, no. I often look and act like this to remind your father how lucky he is to have married."

Satisfied, she went straight to the cookie jar and, giving a cookie to Claudia, she returned to my sick bed. After wavering for an instant, she shrugged one shoulder in an I-might-as-well-get-it-over-with attitude, drew a deep breath, and blurted, "That's good. I'm glad you're not sick because my teacher is making a home visit."

"When?" I struggled to hold back a low scream.

"Well, don't look now, but I think she's coming up the sidewalk."

"You can take me now, Lord," I surrendered. "Please! Before she rings the doorbell." I eyed our surroundings as an educated stranger might do and I saw a dirty three-year-old who certainly, at first glance, seemed neglected; a living room that smelled like a medicine cabinet; and Susan's mother, who was stretched out in her nightgown at 3:45 in the afternoon.

"Quick!" I wheezed, pulling the covers up under my chins. "Wash Claudia's face, fling some deodorizer around, and turn down the heat. It's like a steam bath in here." Doing as she was told, Susan left the room, and I fanned my feverish body with the heavy quilts until she returned with a semi-streaked Claudia on her heels. "I can't find anything to spray with but window cleaner and underarm stuff," she declared. "Do you want me to squirt it around?"

"It's too late now," I sighed as a determined knock was heard at the door. "Let her in, and hope she has plugged sinuses."

Obviously she didn't, because the teacher sailed through the door, her nostrils flaring like open portholes. One whiff, and she stuffed a white lace hankie up her nose. Later, Susan told me not to feel bad. "She stands around in the classroom most of the time with a handkerchief hanging from her nose," she explained.

"Don't get up," the teacher gestured politely as she picked her way delicately across the room. "I'll come to you." Wearing a black skirt, bulky shoes, and a blue blouse that only pooched out because it had buttons, she reminded me a little of a storybook Mary Poppins, sexless, and ranging in age anywhere from thirty-five to eighty-two. The most feminine and pleasant thing about her was the white lace suspended over her stiff mouth. I was trying to pretend I had on a nicely starched housedress instead of a spotted nightgown cut to the navel when Augie sauntered into the room and sat down by a dumbfounded Claudia, who hadn't expected to see Mary Poppins jump out of the pages of her little storybooks. Ordinarily a precocious child, she looked dim-witted sitting there with her dirty face creased with surprise wrinkles. Augie, feeling something wasn't quite right with the world, pawed the air and passed gas. The smell became so overwhelming, the teacher was forced to jab her hanky far back in her nose.

"I'm not fond of dogs," she gasped. "*Or* small children."

"The dog won't hurt you," I promised. "The little girl won't hurt you either." Again I turned my eyes heavenward. "Lord, please keep her from passing out. I don't have the strength to haul her off the floor."

"Are you Mrs. Lueth?" she asked incredulously, picking a couple of cobwebs from her flat blue blouse as she settled down in a chair full of old magazines and cat hair.

"I am," I said weakly, wishing I weren't. Oh, how I longed casually to say that I was a visiting cousin, and that the real Mrs Lueth was off on a gay, whirlwind tour of Europe and wasn't expected back until after the holidays.

"This is my mother," poor Susan said proudly. "And that's my little sister and that's my dog." Claudia blushed and blinked her eyes as if she had a tic; Augie gave a couple of hearty dog grunts; and my nose lit up as a hacking spasm racked my lungs.

"I'm very susceptible to colds," the teacher mumbled, covering her face with both hands. She was perspiring heavily and looking more and more as if she might keel over. "Is it warm in here, or is it me?"

I decided at this point that there was no real reason to be polite and that small talk was a waste of her time and mine; besides, it looked more and more as if one of us was going to faint at any moment. "Why are you here?" I asked bluntly.

"I enjoy visiting my students' homes," she whispered through her knuckles. "It gives me an insight on their classroom performance if I can view the home environment." Poor, poor Susan I thought. "We're doing a unit on the family, and prior to the final test I wanted to see exactly what each student has to draw on from personal experiences. Yours is my last visit." She looked almost happy for a minute. "But I'd really like to meet the entire family."

"My dad isn't home," Susan said. For some reason this didn't seem to surprise the teacher at all.

"Next time, Lord," I hinted, "You might give some thought and consideration to seeing that he *is* here."

"Did you say something?" the teacher asked, drawing a tiny notebook and pencil from her purse. "If you don't mind, I'm going to take notes."

"I was talking to my heavenly Father," I said piously, hoping she would at least have enough kindness left to jot down "Seems religious" in her notes. She sat there for a minute, busily writing, and then suddenly she stood up, shoved notebook and pencil in her purse, snapped it shut, and said, "I'm going now. Possibly I've outstayed my welcome." Her sudden movements sent Claudia scurrying behind a big chair, her face as white as an oyster's. Teacher stood there looking at me as if she expected something that I wasn't prepared to give.

"I'm afraid I can't offer refreshments," I apologized.

"Oh." She looked disappointed.

"I suppose I could rustle up some aspirin and Nyquil."

"No, thank you," she said primly. "If you'll hold the dog, I'll leave now." Susan showed her out. Sadly I said she probably shouldn't plan on passing that class.

Later, when I was feeling much better, I remembered to ask her how she came out on the test. "Did the teacher give you a good grade?"

"The teacher hasn't been to school for a long, long time," Susan grinned. "She's been sick with a bad cold."

"Thank You," I said quietly. My mother always told me prayers would be answered if a person just waited long enough.

Soon I got well enough to walk around the house without stooping, and the children got sick. They were always group-sick in November and caught every communicable disease known to man plus some they invented on their own.

"I've paid for seven hundred sixty-eight immunizations since April. Why are they still breaking out?" Lee complained.

"This is November," I told him. "The children always get sick in November. They do it to keep us in suspense during the holidays. It's as much a part of childhood as training pants and crackerjacks. Children make it a point not to catch anything in the summertime when it's warm and bright and you can air out the house."

"I hope they all get better soon," he said, grabbing his hat, coat, snow boots, and gloves. He went happily from room to room to kiss flushed faces, then aimed a hug in my direction and went out the door, whistling as he climbed into the car and drove away. Most people refused to come into our house during our infectious period—family, friends, and neighbors all refused. After forty-eight hours of confinement, I would've been happy to see Susan's teacher reel up to the door.

I called Helen and begged her to come over for coffee. "I'm sorry," she said, "but I have to stay home today and inventory the canned goods and bottle some water in case of a national emergency. I've been meaning to do this for months, and this is my chance." Her voice sounded hollow. I knew what she was doing. I knew she was holding her hand over the telephone so no germs could squeeze through the little holes.

"Please, Helen. Just for a minute. You won't have to eat anything or stay long."

"God, no, I'm not coming over. I don't want to catch it." I was trapped in a toddler twilight zone. Even my best friend avoided me.

No one was really ill. Just itchy or swollen or slightly achy—and cross, bored, whiny, and nagging. "Where is that Popsicle Man?" Amy cried as she stood before the parted drapes at the picture window, peering out into the ice, snow, and cold wind. "Where is he? I've been waiting so long. Doesn't he know I'm sick?"

"The Popsicle Man doesn't come in November," I told her patiently.

"I bet Marilyn Lorraine's daddy shot him," she said, her lower lip quivering. "He said he was going to shoot him if he didn't stop coming down our street."

"The Popsicle Man doesn't come in November," I repeated sadly, wishing with all my heart that he did. Perhaps *he* would've come inside the house for a cup of coffee and a chat.

Claudia tugged on my shirt. "I'm coloring, Mommy."

"That's nice, dear. What are you coloring?"

"Why, I'm coloring the pretty butterflies on my bedroom walls."

"There are no butterflies on your bedroom walls," I said sweetly.

"There are now, Mom," John explained. "I saw them. They're very big with brown spots, green eyes, and purple antennae. I think they may be hard to wash off." Quickly picking up his artistic baby sister, the two of them went to stand before the picture window with Amy to watch for the Popsicle Man. I went into Claudia's room with a bucket of water and a scrub brush. I found

Mary hiding behind the bed, her little red spots standing out like balloons on her ashen face. "Mommy, Mommy," she screamed, running into my arms. "David's scaring me."

"How could your very own brother scare you?" I stooped down to hug her close. Because of Mary's great imagination, a table lamp often frightened her.

"He said he's going to throw me outside and let the frost bite me."

"Frost doesn't bite little girls," I assured her. I didn't eliminate the possibility that it might take a great chunk out of a certain ten-year-old boy. I suggested she go in with her brother and sisters and look outside. "You might be surprised," I said wistfully. "Maybe he *will* come in November." Returning to the butterflies, I was in the middle of erasing a green eye, when Karen came running into the room. "Something is happening in the bathroom," she said. "David was in there, flushed, and now the stool won't stop gurgling, and there's water all over the floor. I think you'd better come, quick!" Glancing quickly toward the picture window, I checked to see that Mary was still there and not dog-paddling in the sewer, and hurried to the telephone to call the plumber.

"How many are sick?" he asked cautiously.

"This is November," I reminded him. "They are *all* sick." Reluctantly, he agreed to come over, but before he came in he tied a large, antiseptic bandana over his face, which threw Mary into another screaming panic because she thought we were being robbed. She begged her big brother to save her. John, with nothing better to do, stalked the plumber with jabbing fists as he knelt by our bathroom stool, jiggling first this doo-hickey and then that doo-hickey. "This kid's nuts," the plumber said, handing me a bill that would guarantee no new shoes for anyone for six months.

"He's been ill," I apologized weakly. And now he's going to be barefoot for the rest of the winter, I felt like adding, but instead, to get their minds off of being mugged and being called names, I announced that as soon as Mr. Plumber left I would start our evening meal. "We'll have baked chicken, mashed potatoes, and gravy," I said cheerfully.

"But we haven't had lunch," Susan pointed out. "It's still morning."

"What the hell," I said. Letting the plumber out the door, I joined the children at the window, staring out into the fog . . . hoping against hope.

"Here he comes!" Amy pointed to a shivering figure coming from the vicinity of the driveway. "I told you the Popsicle Man would find me."

"See! See!" Claudia jumped up and down, clapping her little hands.

"That's only Daddy," Mary said. "Daddy's home from work early." And it was Daddy all right. He came into the house, stomping snow off his shoes, wearing an I-thought-you-could-use-some-help look and carrying a large brown paper sack. "I bought a treat for my sick kids," he smiled, happily handing out cherry-flavored Popsicles with one left over for me. I'm not too much on Popsicles, but I ate it. It tasted, oh, so sweet; and suddenly November didn't seem so bad after all.

In my opinion, a husband is better than an old Popsicle Man any day.

27
Does the Family
Doctor Ever Lie?

WHEN THE CHILDREN were going through their "This is November, so I'm sick" routine, I spent twenty-two hours a week in the doctor's office. It was my only social life, and I looked forward to it in the same way most women look forward to visiting the beauty parlor. Soft and hard chairs circled the main desk of the waiting room; you could count on bad backs claiming the hard ones and hemorrhoids seeking out the soft. Because the room was quite small, we had no secrets from one another. I relished striking up a conversation with the lady who complained loudly that she had such severe female problems it caused her insides to hang out dangerously; I gave a fascinated David an MYOB glare when he stared intently, trying to pinpoint from whence they hung.

Sharing secrets with the mother of a pale tonsillectomy, I paused long enough to exchange bland recipes with a gall bladder and commented on the perils of icy sidewalks with a broken leg. I often wondered why the nurse didn't serve coffee and cookies. It would've added so much to our enjoyment.

As I ordinarily took the children to the doctor one at a time, we became popular regulars. "Well, hi!" everyone called out as I came through the door for the fourth time that week, leading adorable Claudia, dressed in her

203

Sunday best. The receptionist tipped her pencil in greeting. Taking our family file from its special corner of her desk, she slapped it professionally on top of the others so the doctor would be sure to see it. "Won't be long," she smiled cheerfully. Chair legs scraped as people moved to make room for us. Gall Bladder admired Claudia's frilly outfit and observed that she seemed to have grown since the previous day. I settled down to a relaxing afternoon of diagnosis-and-prognosis gossip while Claudia sat nicely by my side, carefully turning the pages in the Little Golden Books. I was always surprised when the nurse beckoned that it was our turn to see the doctor. Broken Leg raised his crutches in salute and called out, "See you tomorrow," as we went out the door.

Probably I should never have taken all seven of them at the same time.

Yet what could I do? Everyone needed a booster shot and a long-overdue school physical. And because the school nurse had threatened to paste quarantine signs on their backs if I didn't get this done, I didn't hesitate to set up appointments for all seven. The nurse had had the nerve to send home an official demand: "I will no longer accept notes on the back of grocery lists that give approximate dates of inoculations. According to our last communiqué, Mrs. Lueth, John received his polio vaccine twenty-one months before he was born; Mary has had a series of sixteen measle shots since September 1, and your oldest daughter has never been immunized for anything."

A picky lady, that school nurse, I told Lee. He said she was only following the law of the land and that I'd better do something right away if I wanted to keep them in the public-school system. Of course, I wanted to keep them in school. Wouldn't Claudia be entering kindergarten in two years? If God were willing and Lee used some common sense, I'd finally have the house all to myself for a few hours each day. Taking all seven children to the doctor at one time seemed a small price to pay for such a bright future.

"Jesus!" a rheumatic, wrinkled old man cried out as the eight of us hurtled into the office like the Hell's Angels. Tucking hitherto unmoveable joints under his chair, he scrunched down, clutching a battered hat on his lap, as a smiling Claudia walked over to say hello.

"Nice man," she cooed, sinking four little incisors into his gnarled hand.

"She bit me!" he yelled. He began to move about the office like a twenty-one-year-old, stopping before each patient in the room, holding out his hand for examination. "Did you see that? She bit me."

I apologized to the old man, helped him back to his chair, and retrieved his hat from Amy's head. I tried to soothe things by reminding him that if he had to be bitten, where better than a doctor's office? Besides, Claudia hadn't even broken his tough old hide. There wasn't any blood; I saw no reason for him to carry on so.

Sending the three little girls over to the reading corner, I cautioned them not to tear pages out of the books. I asked David to stop hovering over the lady with the droopy insides, told John not to stare at the whimpering old man, who had now enlisted the sympathies of a merry widow with a goiter; I picked out a perfectly healthy, calm-looking middle-aged woman to sit beside. She shot out of her chair as if she were on fire.

"My migraine," she screamed. "What are you doing to my migraine?"

I hadn't done a damn thing, and said so. She went over to huddle with the wimpy old coward and his lady goiter and the three of them whispered about "early graves" and how my children were going to put them there unless they changed doctors. Mary pranced proudly around the office, showing off the squashed bouquet of dusty pheasant, duck and turkey feathers she'd brought along as an afterthought; and four allergy patients wheezed simultaneously. Honestly, I didn't know she had them with her. She was a collector and loved sharing. The sneezers, God bless them, should've been happy she hadn't decided to bring her potpourri of dead October crickets, each interred in its own tissue-wrapped casket. I'd attended every one of their funerals so I knew they were all buried somewhere in her bedroom. Amy was molesting Broken Leg, nagging for a horsey ride on his cast, while her two brothers dueled with his crutches in the middle of the room. Claudia had become bored with terrorizing the old man and cuddled up to a very pregnant young lady. It was obviously a first pregnancy because her husband had accompanied her, and the two of them sat quietly, clasping and unclasping each other's hands as they watched what could be their very own parental future unroll before their eyes.

"You didn't tell me about this kind of thing when you begged for a baby." The young husband seemed despondent, a bit frightened and quite cross. "I told you I wasn't ready for fatherhood."

"You certainly seemed eager enough to participate," his wife snapped back. And enjoyed every minute of it, too, I thought to myself, but held my tongue. Gathering the three little girls to my side, I told John and David they should go outside and stand in the snow until the doctor came. Throughout the afternoon, Karen and Susan had been wandering about the office reading the doctor's credentials on the wall and pretending they were eighteen and nineteen years old.

"Did you know our doctor specializes in something called *hysterectomy?*" Susan asked, looking puzzled. "What's a hysterectomy?"

"Your mother doesn't have it," a newcomer, Mr.

Hardhat, who'd been nursing a sore elbow and threatening to go sit on an icy scaffold where it was safe, said. He chuckled at his own earthy humor.

"Can you get one, Mom?"

"I suppose I could if I had the right symptoms," I said.

"I'll be glad to tell you what to say," chimed in the plump Lady Goiter.

"I can't stand this stress," sniveled a jumpy gentleman, who'd spent most of the afternoon bent over with stomach pains. "I'm leaving." He jerked open the office door, nearly knocking down the doctor, who was stepping over the threshold with a subdued John and David in tow.

"You'll never get well that way," the doctor called out.

"I'll take my chances and drink milk," said the man. He disappeared into the cold air.

When Amy saw the doctor, she remembered why she was there and set up a loud howl, soon joined by Claudia. They stood, open-mouthed, in the middle of the room. The young mother-to-be clutched the doctor's hand and cried, "I think I'm going into labor. Will you help me please, doctor?" Her husband strained right along with her, looked me up and down, and said, "My mother told me I should have gone into the priesthood instead of accounting." The two of them disappeared into the back offices.

"Shut your mouths if you know what's good for you," John warned his little sisters. "That doctor's a mean one." A shudder ran through his whole body; David looked unusually pale.

"What did that doctor say to you?" I asked him.

"I don't think I should tell you."

"Tell me. I'm your mother."

"You know those squishy, pickled things he has in jars all over his examining room?" John asked. I knew what he was talking about because Lee had mentioned once that they reminded him of the dills I'd put up the year before, intending to give them to our neighbors at Christmastime. "He said they were really little kids that didn't behave when they came to the doctor. Does a doctor ever lie, Mom?"

"Once in a while," I told him, rubbing his back to calm him down a little. "Once in a while, even a doctor lies." I could say that in good faith because I was told twice I was suffering from a nervous stomach and eventually we named them Mary and David. "But I don't think we should take any chances." And we didn't.

From that day on, we were *all* good when we went to the doctor.

28
Taking a Trip with Mickey Bat

A WEEK LATER, unfortunate circumstances and a bit of tough meat threw me directly into the arms of the tooth fairy's best friend—our family dentist. For some strange reason, our children didn't mind going to the dentist. They crawled right up into his chair, spread their little mouths like salad tongs, and spit dead center into the bowl without being told twice. When it was my turn, however, I was terrified. It dated back to my own childhood days when dentists had whiskey-sour breath and used drills that sounded like machine guns. I could remember sitting there for what seemed like hours with a hairy hand rammed down my throat. Lee told me I should be ashamed of being such a coward; that modern-day equipment had made going to the dentist as painless as a manicure. "A swish, a whish, and you're done," he said.

"If his hand slips and he drills a hole in my tongue, that's it forever." I wanted pity, not logic. "I'll never be able to speak in whole sentences again."

"Quit worrying. You'll be fine. You're overreacting."

Overreacting, be damned, I was scared out of my mind. Easy for him to be nonchalant. He had teeth like a steel comb and only went to the dentist once a year to have a good cleaning. My teeth had a tendency to crumble if I pressed a marshmallow to my lips, and cavities crept through my roots like ivy. "What if he sews my mouth shut by mistake?"

"He won't," Lee laughed, "no matter how great the temptation. He's a professional. His reputation is excellent, and you've known him since he was in college." Yes, and somehow I wished I'd followed his academic career a little more closely and sent him a nice present when he graduated from dental school instead of briskly shaking his hand and clapping him on the back one day when I met him on the street. How did I know he was going to buy my root-canal records when our old dentist retired?

"He's probably dreading this more than you are," Lee said. To take my mind off of my appointment the next day, he invited me to dinner. "Sort of a 'last supper,'" he grinned. After three glasses of white wine, I leaned over to confide in the people sitting at the next table that I was entering surgery the next day and that this, perhaps, was my final full day on earth. They looked properly sympathetic and gave me the comfort I'd been seeking from my husband, until he told them I was only going to the dentist; then they turned their backs and would look our way only when they thought I wasn't watching.

Later that evening, while we were sitting up in bed trying to decide whether to eat a bowl of cornflakes or make love, Lee volunteered to stay home from work and take care of things around the house so I could get a good rest when I got home from the dentist. I told him I wasn't sure I was going, and he said, of course you're going, and turned over and went to sleep. I hardly slept a wink. The combination of fear, cornflakes, and white wine kept me wide awake. When morning came, I hopped sleepily from bed and scurried about, tidying my desk, watering the artificial flowers, mending, looking

up words in the dictionary, brushing the dog. As I ran
the brush softly and slowly through Augie's fur, his suspicious eyes followed every move I made. I seldom spoke
to him during the day, let alone touched him. These
warm attentions were more than he could bear and he
twisted away to hide under the bed. I rang up the dentist and told him I was into some really important stuff
at home. "I'll probably be a bit late," I said gravely.

"Don't be," he replied.

"Would it do any good to tell you I've changed my
mind?"

"No," he said as he hung up.

Lee kissed my soon-to-be-maimed lips and said I
should just go on and get it over with. Reluctantly and
with great sorrow, I hugged my babies and left the
house. I knew I couldn't keep driving around the block
forever; when I finally decided I could stand on my own,
I parked the car and walked into the dentist's office with
my mouth cooperatively wide open, determined not
to cry.

"I'm yours," I trembled.

"Don't worry," the dentist said quietly. Taking my
hand tenderly, he led me into his office. "We'll use
happy gas. You'll be completely relaxed and absolutely
uninhibited."

Oh, my God!

Pushing me into a leather chair, he told me all I'd
have to do was think about nice things and he'd do all
the hard work. "Close your eyes, sink back, and let
yourself float," he suggested. "You'll be drifting in no
time at all." I hated to burst his bubble but floating was
going to be tough for someone my size. Screwing up my
face, I chanted "Float, damn body, float!" and I opened
my eyes to see if I'd drifted anywhere important.
Screaming, I sat straight up in the chair.

"I haven't touched you," the dentist roared. "I only

put a bib around your neck. There is absolutely no excuse for yelling like that."

"There are bats on your ceiling."

"Not bats. It's Mickey Mouse in a Superman cape. I
put him there for the little tots. They like it. They laugh
out loud and open their mouths wide. I'm calling your
husband."

"Please, don't." I grabbed the tail of his white coat.
"I'd rather take my chances with Mickey Bat, thank
you." I leaned back to let him have his way with me.

For the next forty-five minutes or so, my life cen-
tered on scurrying movements and lots of suction.
Through a pinkish-green haze, I heard "Here it comes!"
"Got it!" "Whoops!" "A little more gauze here, please,"
and "Damnit." Frankly, I couldn't have cared less. I
wasn't in the least bit intimidated by all this. I was
sucking happy gas like it was a chocolate soda and having the time of my life. At the exact moment that my
tooth popped out I was afloat over the California coast
with Robert Redford on my heels and we were headed,
downwind, toward old Mexico.

"Olé!" I gurgled.

"Did you say something?" the weary, somewhat dis-
traught dentist asked. I shook my head, and smiled, and
smiled and smiled a gaping smile. I hadn't had this
much fun in years. Talk about a trip. I was sorry to see
it all end, but eventually all good things do; and I was
dusted off, released from my bib, given a fair shot of
oxygen, and brought back into the real world. But not
before Mickey Bat winked at me.

"See you next week," he whispered, dipping a wing.

I could hardly wait.

29

My God! You Can't Burn Lettuce

WHEN OUR SECONDHAND HONEYMOON refrigerator emitted its last icy croak, it was hard for Lee and me to accept the fact that this dear old friend had actually passed away. We'd proudly bought it with our first combined paycheck and done everything but sit inside it and manipulate the little electric light by hand to keep it going. When it shuddered and produced more heat than the furnace, Lee rearranged wires—so that it iced up so badly it froze cookie dough into hailstones and the cabbage came out like giant green snowballs. When I dipped a knife into the jelly jar it bent to a crazy angle; the orange juice was like hot soup. However, the morning the refrigerator leaned dangerously to the left and spit fumes that smelled like rotten eggs, we knew it was a goner.

"I was going to surprise you for Christmas," Lee called from his office, "but I don't think we can wait. In about fifteen minutes there should be a new frost-free refrigerator delivered. I hope you like the color." Wow! Who cared about color? It could be light purple for all I cared.

Letting a good nip of winter air into the kitchen, I stepped aside as the delivery man maneuvered his dolly through the door. "Good God, lady, that is a tall refrigerator." He stared at the corner where Secondhand Westinghouse Rose stood. "I've never seen one that stood seven foot before." Actually, he was exaggerating. My old refrigerator was only a regulation five foot six, but the stuff accumulated under it made it seem much taller. I seldom had time to clean under things and really hadn't given it a thought for months—or maybe years. When I did think of it, I was afraid that if I moved it, it would collapse. I'd gotten used to having a refrigerator that grew faster than our children, but the man from the appliance store seemed quite overcome.

When he pried the refrigerator away from the wall, I nearly passed out. Popping out in plain sight were several dust balls large enough to use as pillows, a shriveled biscuit or two, and some Monopoly money. Mixed in with old turkey bones and loose change was a slightly dopey cricket, turned pale and gray and gulping for fresh air. I thought to myself, Better hurry, Mr. Cricket, or Mary will have another corpse to lay away in a Kleenex shroud.

"If anyone deserved a new refrigerator, you did lady." The man worked his way back into the house, wheeling an Avocado King beauty. Bending to fit the plug into the proper socket, he stepped back and spread his hands proudly as a soft, harmonious mechanical hum filled the room. It was gorgeous. I reached out to stroke its sparkling, unchipped surface. I'd barely touched its cool sides when a rumbling caused me to snatch my hand away and grab the delivery man's arm. "Have I killed it already?" I cried.

"Oh, no, ma'am," he laughed. "That's just the automatic ice maker kicking in and getting ready to make ice."

"I didn't know I was getting an ice maker." I sat down hard in a nearby chair to catch my breath. Never, in all of my life, did I ever think that I, Shirley Lueth, would own an automatic ice maker.

"I'll say this for your husband—when he finally breaks down, he doesn't skimp. This is a real jewel." The delivery man, looking proud that he'd made the slovenly housekeeper so happy, smiled gratefully. I resisted the urge to dance across the floor and tickle him under his chin; instead I invited him to join me in a cup of coffee and a couple of cookies. He looked at the giant hailstones nesting on the counter and politely declined. "I have a wife and three children," he said quietly to no one in particular. "I'll just go back to work now."

My gratitude to Lee knew no bounds. For days I did nothing but sit and watch the precious ice maker churn out perfectly formed cold crescents. "How many today, Mom?" the children called out when they came home from school.

"At last count I had one thousand, seven hundred forty-nine," I said breathlessly. "Isn't it marvelous!" I called Helen and asked her if she wouldn't like to come over and watch ice drop. She said she didn't think so. For a few days Augie hung around; then he, too, grew bored and left me. I threw open the door victoriously each time the mechanism spit. Running my hands through the cubes as if they were diamonds, I tried to ignore the fact I was spending most of my waking hours with frozen fingertips. Lee told me I was being a little silly and that he was getting tired of finding nothing in our deep freeze but bags full of ice. "It isn't normal to be that thrilled over ice cubes," he said. Maybe not, but I was positive the refrigerator was proud too. For some reason it looked taller.

During the past year or two I'd been sharing kitchen duties with Karen, who had volunteered to help with the cooking. This worked out well because Karen organized recipes much as she did her dresser drawers; everything had its place. She even hung up the dish towels instead of slinging them over the back of a chair. Her appreciation for our new refrigerator was as deep as mine. "Now," she said, "we won't have any more frozen butter." Humming quietly, she spread nineteen pieces of toast with quick strokes without mutilating the bread. Claudia, bless her heart, had never eaten a piece of toast that wasn't shredded and punctured from knife wounds and we had a terrible time persuading her that it wasn't dangerous to eat square bread. Karen vowed that if she could help it not one drop of chocolate syrup would ever mar the inside of that Avocado King as long as it lived.

Susan, at that time, hadn't developed many kitchen skills. She could whip up a mean bologna sandwich and stir Kool-Aid, but she had a tendency to spill and once in a while she put the sugar bowl in the oven. The new refrigerator had appealed to her momentarily but she wasn't bewitched. She was more interested in amusing the three little girls with doll weddings and doll adultery. It was nothing for Susan to arrange a society wedding for Barbie and Ken on Tuesday, only to have a wanton Barbie run off in a jeep with G.I. Joe on Wednesday. Poor preppy Ken in his sissy tennis togs had little chance when Macho Joe showed up in his sweaty army fatigues. Amy, Mary, and Claudia clapped their hands in delight when Susan turned Barbie into a feisty little sexpot and the dolly triangle churned out torrid love stories in much the same manner as the icemaker did the precious ice cubes. "I'm teaching them about men," Susan explained. "Don't you think it's as important as learning to cook?"

Karen said *her* way made more sense. "My Home Ec. teacher said the way to a man's heart was through his stomach. She made us learn to cook."

"Oh, ours tried at the beginning," Susan told us as she slipped a bikini no bigger than a pin head onto Barbie's eternally slim hips, "but Sarah Ann complained that all the burned casseroles made the school smell like an outhouse, so we quit and learned about sex and stuff like that." Sarah Ann was Helen's oldest daughter and probably had been taught at her mother's knee that babies came from belly buttons and that prime rib was only a nickname for Eve. Sarah Ann probably knew more about cooking than the teacher anyway, having spent three sessions at gourmet-cooking camp. It was sex she was interested in . . . not soufflés.

Helen went to the principal and told him Sarah Ann was learning to talk dirty in school, so eventually the teacher had to do something constructive about cooking and Susan was assigned a project that included planning, preparing, and serving an entire meal by herself. She traded a weary Barbie in for a spatula and I promised to help her, but in all fairness I told her she should do most of it by herself. "Daddy will be so proud of you."

"Not when he finds out what we're having to eat." Susan twisted her long hair nervously. "We're having Pigs in a Blanket and Cowboy Cookies."

"No one eats Pigs in a Blanket for dinner," Lee protested. For some odd reason he'd expected pot roast. "And the last time I ate Cowboy Cookies my insides felt spurred. Can't you think of something else?" Susan was frantic. It was bad enough that she had to spend more than five minutes in the kitchen; now she was disappointing a hungry father. "You do what the teacher told you," I said. "I'll take care of your father." I knew I was no Barbie but that didn't mean I didn't have a trick or two to fall back on when necessary.

Ordinarily it takes about fifteen minutes flat to prepare Pigs in a Blanket. All you need do is split a few wieners, ram in some cheese, tie it up with slices of bacon, stick a toothpick or two in at random, and put them in the oven for 350 degrees until the cheese melts and the bacon cooks. It took Susan nearly four hours.

She had several good fits and used nearly every pot and pan in the house.

"I can't cut them! I can't cut them!" she screamed, waving a heavy cleaver above the dozen or so hot dogs lined up on the counter. "I can't even make a dent."

"You have to thaw them first," I patiently reminded her.

"Oh," Susan drooped. "Our dumb teacher didn't mention that. She didn't say anything about frozen wienies." Flapping the sharp knife over her head, she marched across the kitchen floor, causing Augie to soar out of the room like an eagle. "She doesn't tell us anything. All she says is 'set a pretty table . . . set a pretty table.' She didn't say one word about taking the food out of the freezer. I don't care how pretty I set the table, Daddy won't eat frozen hot dogs." She was right. So I told her to forget the meat and fix the salad. "By the time the salad is prepared, the hot dogs will be thawed."

"I've already thrown the salad away."

"Why?"

"I burned it."

"My God. You can't burn lettuce."

"I did."

"But you must have a salad," I insisted. "Your suggestion sheet says that well-balanced meals always include salad."

"We're having salad." Susan stuck her chin out defiantly. "I fixed chocolate chips. I'm going to write down 'tossed' on my report; but we're having chocolate chips."

"But you won't be telling the truth."

"So I'll toss in some radishes," she said stubbornly. "That should do it." It certainly should.

"Daddy will love it," I gagged.

"We aren't having cookies either. They shriveled up and I threw them on the floor and Augie ate them." So much for the Cowboys, I thought, gone to their last roundup in a hairy stomach.

"What are you making for dessert?"

"Fruit Roll," and Susan busily collected a bunch of oranges, apples, and bananas in a large bowl.

"That sounds nice. How do you fix it?"

"Easy. You just roll the fruit across the floor and call it dessert."

"But what will your teacher say to that?" I asked in a shocked voice.

"What she doesn't know won't hurt her," Susan grinned. I knew right then I had nothing to teach this daughter of ours. Heavens, hadn't I lived by that same kitchen philosophy for years? Probably Susan would turn out to be as good a cook as I am.

30

The World's Sweetest Feeling

I SAT UP NIGHT AFTER NIGHT making Christmas surprises for my family, each stitch taken in a kind of desperate love. I wondered how Nebraska's pioneer women had managed to hand-knit every inch of warm clothing on their family's backs. A sweater took me two years of futile tangling and untangling, and then it was regarded as a poor substitute for the real thing and only worn when I forced it over their heads. Karen claimed she was growing tired of climbing on the school bus looking as if she were attending a funeral because her mother bought every skein of yarn on sale and every bit of it was either coal black or a deep mournful purple. And because these late-night sewing sessions left me cross-eyed and tired early in the morning, Lee insisted that I come to bed at a decent hour like an ordinary person and stop sitting up all night sewing and knitting for the children. "You're a good mommy," he smiled, "but I miss you and can hardly sleep when you aren't beside me."

Who then, I wondered, was doing all the snoring I heard from our bedroom?

Lee probably didn't realize that I used those hours to think, to dream, and to remember. It was so very quiet (if you didn't count the snoring), no one stole my scissors, and Helen didn't drop in to see if I'd cleaned the bathroom. It was my time. I could listen to the kind of music I liked on the stereo, I didn't have to nod politely as Mary told me the story of Alice in Wonderland from start to finish, and I knew where each and every member of my family was and that they were safe, well, and asleep. For the moment I had everything . . . and everyone . . . under complete control. Every mother knows it's the world's sweetest feeling.

With a hot cup of cocoa at my side, a warm afghan over my knees, and Andy Williams crooning in the background, I curled up with my dreams. While the snow piled up outside, my memory took wing to a hot July afternoon in southern Illinois. I was ten years old and walking barefoot to the public library or cheating the kid next door out of his marbles. As a child I'd alternated between being the toughest chick on the block and a quivering mass of feminine Jell-O whenever a boy looked my way. With pigtails down to my hips and imaginary silver slippers on my feet, I apparently danced to the tune of a different drummer. I wasn't very pretty, and I had scabs on my knees most of the time.

Sometimes I led symphony orchestras with an invisible baton as the pounding music of the console radio bounced off the walls of the living room . . . or I was a schoolteacher with a classroom of obedient paper dolls lined up on my bedspread . . . when the urge to get outside was strong I could pitch a baseball far enough to please my father. I wore shoes only when forced to visit relatives, to go to church, or when the weather warranted. I yearned for a pair of shiny black patent-leather pumps instead of the sturdy brown oxfords that were half-soled so many times, I really never knew just how tall I was. (Smiling to myself, I thought of our own five daughters and how they kicked and moaned because they were made to wear black patent-leather

shoes until they were teenagers when all they ever
really wanted was a pair of army boots.) I had freckles
and square hands that turned into clumsy oafs whenever my mother tried to teach me to tat.

"I can't do this, Mama," I complained bitterly, glancing over at my sister Virginia who was dropping yards
of delicate, icy-flaked lace from her shuttle. I was surrounded by wads of dirty white knots and the shuttle
did somersaults in my palms.

"You give up much too easily, Shirley," my mother
sighed. "You could do anything you wanted if you set
your mind to it."

I didn't learn to tat. However, armed with this maternal advice, I set my mind to capturing the heart,
soul, and body of the handsomest sixteen-year-old in
Union County. Of course, I was only ten, so I had no
idea what I'd do with him if I caught him, but I hung
like a morning glory vine on the iron fence surrounding
his house and watched as he mowed the lawn. Even
with grass stains on his britches he looked luscious. I
followed him to the grocery store, to his friend's house,
and to the soda fountain. My senses soared so high they
brushed clouds when he winked and said "Hi, kid," but
they plunged to the ground the next day when he asked
his mother to do something about the little girl who
hung on the fence. I dreamed of the day when he'd ask
me to be his wife. And one day, a few years later, he
actually did and I regretfully said no. Even at an early
age, I knew that a good marriage wasn't based on blind
worship, especially if I were the one expected to do the
worshiping. But that was another memory; and, as I listened to the dear and patient man snuffling in the bedroom down the hall, I thanked him for showing up when
I desperately needed someone to live with for the rest of
my life.

But where, I thought, had my luck been the day

Tatty Virginia dared me to snitch the pineapple upside-down cake cooling in the pantry? Ordinarily, the naughtiest thing this precious sister could do was to crawl in a dark closet and stick her tongue out at our dad when he was fourteen blocks away from home with his back turned. When she suggested I steal the cake, I was so astonished by her daring that I didn't hesitate but stealthily sneaked through the kitchen, snatched it up, and ran out the back door. She was waiting in a grove of fruit trees behind the house, and the two of us spent the afternoon devouring every sweet crumb.

To this day I have no idea what our mother intended doing with that "company cake" because she never once mentioned its disappearance. A sensible woman, she waited, knowing full well the gluttons would give themselves away in time, and we did, throwing up consistently all that night and the next day; our pale yellow-green complexions shouted our guilt. Mama only held our heads and wiped our brows, smiling slightly as she said we'd soon feel better.

Between nauseous moans, Virginia and I took a blood oath that we'd never touch pineapple upside-down cake again; just to be in the same room with the thick syrupy smell of baking pineapple combined with brown sugar brought sick tears to my eyes. My mother kept our secret—but, for the rest of our days together as a family, and years later at each reunion, our sweet mama managed to serve this deadly dessert as the specialty of her house. It cured me of stealing anything. I believed it when Mother told me stealing was a crime never to be forgotten by the thief. "Perhaps you'll get by with it," she warned, "but in your heart you'll pay." The pineapple upside-down cake hadn't affected my heart but it had certainly played hell with my stomach; so, though the anatomy was wrong, Mama was right. She usually was.

When my parents moved to California, I'd been married a number of years and was a mommy myself, but this didn't mean I still didn't listen to my mother. Her advice filled my life in the form of detailed weekly letters, punctuated perfectly and containing large exclamation marks. When she wrote "Trim your doggie's nails! It's for his health's sake!" I sat on an astonished Augie and pried off claw after claw, leaving him with toes like marshmallows, dripping tiny bloodlets all over the carpet. In time, when he saw me lift up a pair of manicure scissors from the dressing table, he rolled his eyes, fled, and wouldn't come home until we'd advertised at least three times over the radio for: Lost Dog with Black Collar; answers to the name of Augie; has slightly bloody feet and no toenails.

I used the nonchalant potty-training methods Grandma sent from California and patiently changed fourteen dozen wet panties every day of my life, all the while keeping a sunny smile on my face and good thoughts of Mama in my mind. Suspicious of her methods but thinking she knew what she was talking about, I carried on until the day Claudia reached over for the baby powder, sprinkled herself liberally, and then handed *me* the safety pins. I turned mean and nasty and trained her in eight hours. And I never did tell Mama how I did it, but she bragged that Claudia was the brightest grandchild any grandmother had ever seen.

When Mama wrote about breast-feeding, it sounded so simple: "It's not messy! No expensive formulas! No bottles to sterilize and pack about! It's so good for baby! It's Nature's Way!" Unfortunately, Mama had no idea that Nature and I had parted company long ago.

I did fine while I was in the maternity ward at the hospital. Regularly the nurses brought a rested Mommy and equally rested baby, and I was as contented as Bossy the Cow, while our babies gained weight and spit little milk bubbles on their clothing.

The minute I entered the front door of our house, I dried up like puffed wheat.

"Stress can sour!" Mama wrote back when I sobbed out my problem in my own weekly letter. Again her theory was correct, but she didn't say what to do with the other six children hanging over me as I pretended to be a delicious milk carton eight or nine times a day. Somehow Mama skipped over that and continued to recommend that I "Relax!" I tried, but invariably the baby's hunger cry touched off the telephone, doorbell, sibling quarrels, and screeches from someone whose fingers were closed in the toy box. This, combined with Augie's constant limping and moaning, caused my milk to turn to vinegar; my poor baby looked up with surprised eyes at the mother who would offer such a meal. When I complained, Mama wagged her pencil and warned me not to show my dinners in public.

She had no worry on that count. Modesty was my middle name. I huddled behind the buffet to feed our baby. Any approaching footsteps caused me to scrunch up in a persimmon position; there were so many towels, blankets, and washcloths draped about my person that the baby had difficulty drawing a deep breath.

Young mothers today seem to have worked this all out . . . but then they didn't have my mother to call on when they needed help.

31

Make It Tonight—
Wear It Tomorrow

"MY SEWING MACHINE has become arthritic," I told Lee during what he was referring to as my annual "nesting" period. "When once it went 'whir-whir,' it now goes 'rucka-rucka'! I haven't used it in weeks and it feels neglected. But that's going to change. I'm turning over a new leaf."

"God," Lee sighed. "What now?"

"Will I have to keep my friends out of the house while you're going through this, Mother?" Karen was helping me clear away the Saturday lunch dishes and hoping maybe we'd spice up a dull afternoon ahead by fighting. "Like I did when you were going to can all of our food and wore the double boiler on your head because you were afraid of the pressure cooker?"

"It's nothing like that. I'm simply going to make every stitch of clothing we wear from now on—just like the Pioneer Mothers."

Lee said he thought my late-night knitting and gift-making sessions were making me punchy.

"Well, I won't wear it . . . no matter what it is," John shrieked.

"Neither will I!" David agreed. Obviously, they were remembering the time I'd tried saving money by making their underclothes. The fact that they were the only two boys in school, perhaps in the whole world, whose flies opened in the wrong direction had been not only awkward but most embarrassing. Lee tried soothing their hurt feelings by telling them they were lucky I hadn't sewed them shut completely. It was a long time before my sons trusted me after that, so I promised on my honor that I wouldn't make underwear. They lost interest and went outside to play football.

Until I became a wife and mother I'd never touched a sewing machine. I didn't make doll-baby clothes when I was a child or work on 4H projects to model at the state fair like my sisters. I didn't even take home economics until the school system made me—and after I set my hair on fire the day it was my turn to light the oven, the teacher wrote "Not recommended" on my schedule, and I never had to go near that department again. But when I married, and a budget was slapped in my hand along with the hugs and kisses that ultimately produced the seven children at our house, I took up sewing as a serious business. I thought that if pure enthusiasm had anything to do with it, I could turn out new wardrobes for everyone with one hand stitched behind my back. And I continued to try and explain to Lee that my sewing machine could be the most economical appliance I owned.

"How can you say that?" he shook his head. "You spend sixty dollars for material, come home, rip it up, and stuff it in a drawer. Then you go out and spend another sixty dollars for the dress you couldn't make in the first place. That's economical?"

"You don't understand," I told him. "I'm through doing that. I've found a whole new way to sew. It's all in the pattern." And I showed him the large, black letters on the dress pattern I'd just bought that said "Make It Tonight—Wear It Tomorrow!"

"See that!" I said triumphantly. "It's simple. I'm going to make it tonight, and wear it tomorrow."

"Ha!"

"Don't you believe me?"

"Perhaps if you lived in Lapland, I might."

Puzzled, I asked him what that had to do with anything. I didn't even know where Lapland was.

"In Lapland the night lasts for nine months. Possibly that would give you enough sewing time." Chuckling to himself, he picked up Claudia and the two of them went in to watch cartoons on television.

That evening I warned everyone that after dinner Mother would be very busy sewing and wanted no interference. "I won't be available to take anyone to the library, to help with homework, or read fairy tales. Direct all of these requests to your father." At 7:00 P.M. I cleared the dining-room table and prepared a cutting surface.

At 7:15 I looked for my scissors.

At 7:25 I put on my coat, hat, overboots, and mittens and went across the street to borrow Helen's scissors. "They're my best ones," she said, "and I just had them sharpened. Please try to take care of them."

At 7:30 I removed my coat, hat, overboots, and mittens.

At 7:35 I looked for my straight pins.

At 7:45 I went upstairs and removed 250 of my straight pins from Karen's bulletin board.

At 7:55 I told her if she ever took my straight pins again I'd flatten her.

At 8:00 P.M. I had a cup of hot tea to pull myself together.

At 8:01 I laid the pattern out on the material, pinned it carefully, and stepped back to admire my work. I then noticed I hadn't included front facings. There was no room on the material for front facings. Were they important? I consulted the pattern. They were very important.

At 8:15 I unfolded, refolded, unpinned, repinned, marked, matched, and notched.

At 8:30 I answered the telephone. "No, she isn't here," I said politely. "She went to the store with her father to buy thumbtacks. Yes, I'll have her call you."

At 8:31, checking the front facings, I found they fit beautifully, but left no room for the pockets. Were pockets important? No. I had nothing important to put in pockets.

At 8:40 I answered the telephone. "No, she isn't back. Good-bye."

At 8:41 I took the first cut with Helen's sharp scissors and sheared off 60 percent of the belt. Is a belt important? Hell, no.

At 9:00 P.M. I sat down with a cup of hot tea and two aspirin.

At 9:01 I answered the telephone. "Don't call here again!" I yelled. "But it's only me," my sister Audrey said. "Are you sewing again?"

From 9:05 until 10:00, I cut and cut and cut with Helen's now very dull scissors, until my fingers were sore.

At 10:01 I decided tear stains would not show on material after good laundering.

At 10:05, ignoring the telephone, I let it ring its fool head off; gathering pattern, material, pin cushion, and Helen's choppy scissors, I marched into the sewing room.

At 10:07 I carefully set up the ironing board and plugged in the iron.

At 10:08 I knocked the iron to the floor and smashed it to smithereens.

At 10:09 I put on coat, hat, snow boots, and mittens.

At 10:10 I rapped on Helen's door to beg for her iron. Ray answered the door wearing a bright orange-and-yellow satin kimono. He had a guilty look on his face and his eyes seemed funny. He said something like, what in God's name was I doing ironing at this time of night? and thrust the iron into the pit of my stomach. I wished him pleasant dreams and wished I were dead.

At 10:18 I stitched four darts, pressed them, and they were gorgeous. I was happy to be alive.

At 10:19 I discovered that the gorgeous darts were on the wrong side of the fabric and stood up over my breast like tiny bird wings.

At 10:20 I scanned a fashion magazine to see if anyone was wearing their clothes wrong side out. They weren't.

At 10:25 I tore out four gorgeous darts and replaced them with four not-so-gorgeous, crooked ones.

At 10:40 I pinned the fronts together at the undercollar and stitched the center back seam. The neckline was now carefully sewed under the section labeled Armpit.

From 10:40 until 10:59 I ripped stitches, kicked the ironing board, pounded the sewing machine.

At 11:00 P.M. I said the heck with it, sat down, ignored tea bags, and poured a cold beer. It tasted pretty good. Had another.

At 11:02 Lee came into the room and said if I was just going to sit there getting drunk, he was going to bed.

At 11:03 I looked up happily and said, "Good night, dear . . . sleepy tight!"

At 11:04 I attacked the project with an entirely new outlook.

At 11:05 fourteen miles of side seams were sewn up; the bobbin thread had run out after the second mile.

At 11:06 I rewound the bobbin.

At 11:07 I took my eyes from the little round witch for only a second; the thread wrapped around the spindle beneath, and the bobbin flew into the cat's dish.

At 11:08 I looked longingly at the refrigerator.

At 11:09 I renamed the bobbin.

At 11:10 I pledged never to call it this in the presence of the children.

At 11:11 the pattern indicated it was time to set in the sleeves. I could not find the sleeves.

From 11:12 until 11:21 I hunted for the sleeves. Are sleeves important?

At 11:22 I went to the refrigerator and shouted, "Who needs sleeves!"

At 11:30 I broke the needle on the zipper teeth.

At 11:31 I replaced the needle.

At 11:40 I broke the second needle on the zipper teeth.

At 11:41 I replaced the needle.

At 11:42 I renamed the zipper. Much, much worse than the bobbin. I even surprised myself. Pledged never to say this in presence of *anyone!*

At 11:43 I broke my third and last needle on the zipper teeth.

At 11:44 I picked up the zipper and placed it gently in the garbage can.

From 11:45 until 11:59, I laid my head down on the sewing machine and cried my eyes out.

At midnight I packed my bags and prepared to leave for Lapland.

32

Little Billy Blue Dot Gets into Trouble

IT TOOK ME three weeks and four days to finish my "make it tonight—wear it tomorrow" dress. If you overlooked the crooked darts, absent pockets and belt, and the substitution of snaps for a ridiculous zipper, it didn't look half bad.

"It hangs funny, Mom," Karen said.

"So I'll slant when I walk," I answered sharply, determined to wear something I'd worked so hard to make. But I'd forgotten to reckon with the personality of such a dress. After all of its birthing hardships, it was as determined as I was. The material, smooth as satin when I bought it, turned into thousands of wrinkled love nests for its erotic thread; two hours after I hung it up it was two sizes smaller and had changed colors.

"I can't wear this," I cried. "I'll look just like I crawled out of Augie's bed." Lee had come into the bedroom and found me slumped over with what was obviously a brown cloth prune clutched in my hands. We were having guests for dinner and I was running late. He'd showered, shaved, spit on his shoes, had two martinis, and watched a rerun on television. Reaching for my dress, he offered to shake out the wrinkles.

"Please, please, don't squeeze the dress," I pleaded. "You'll only make it worse."

"Why should I squeeze? he ogled. "You aren't in it." Two martinis and clean shoes had driven the man absolutely mad. "So wear something else."

Sadly I told him there was nothing else, unless you counted my half slip or his good suit.

"I'll set up Helen's iron," he offered. After burning my elbow to the bone, the dress was rendered partially passable, but the magic was gone. I never trusted that dress again, and, even though Brown Wrinkled Rear eventually became one of my nicest dresses and accompanied me to several weddings, christenings, and bridal showers, it still had to be ironed every fifteen minutes and I soon grew tired of leaning to the left whenever I walked into a room.

Carried over from my college days was the rather ridiculous habit of naming my clothes. "Toss me Sexy Sweater," I would call out to my roommate Jayne. She knew exactly which one I meant. She knew it was the pink angora with the puffy sleeves that had caused our gentle-born housemother to switch from cocoa to bourbon in the middle of the afternoon. I shared Galloping Green with my sorority sisters; it became our sorority's favorite skirt. Galloping was a pleated affair that had outrun and outswung every fraternity pledge at Southern Illinois University. Its reputation was far more lurid than the hips doing the swinging but, for a time, Galloping Green was so busy she was never in the closet.

Even though Lee thought I was delirious, I continued to name my clothing after we were married. Take Old Blue, for instance. Old Blue was a plain jacket and skirt that had flown to Boston, kicked up her heels at a wedding dance, and walked around the block to a Tupperware party. Not too glamorous but very versatile.

"You're not wearing that suit again?" Susan groaned when it was my turn to attend a parent-teacher conference.

"Why not? Old Blue is dependable. Old Blue is comfortable. Old Blue is good."

"Old Blue is also ugly," she said. Poor Old Blue hung its buttons in shame; it took a trip to the dry cleaner's to bring it out of its thready doldrums.

Marvy Mauve was one of my favorites. Never mind that she was the color of a tired dish rag. It was always exciting to wear Marvy Mauve because I never knew what tricks she had up her seamy sleeves or when she might fall apart and leave me standing in the middle of a crowded room in my underwear. When I was least expecting it, she often opened up with a seductive split somewhere between the waistline and the hemline; she ate safety pins like whipping cream. Her ruffles dipped into punch bowls and her bodice popped open at the slightest provocation. Lee refused to be seen in public with me when I was wearing Marvy Mauve.

Dear Fat Pink was the all-time, all-encompassing, all-American maternity dress. There wasn't a tuck in the whole ton. I hid millions of calories behind Dear Fat Pink and continued to lift her out of the closet with a crane even after Claudia's birth. With a pair of pearls wrapped around her neckline, she was ready for anything and so was I. Lee wasn't overly fond of Fat Pink.

Wee Winnie Woolen clung to me like someone was going to rip her from my body. She rolled up around my waist, clutched me under the chin so tight I couldn't turn my head; and when I crossed my legs, Wee Winnie recoiled in embarrassed shame and crept nervously toward my armpits. No amount of tugging and pulling could reassure Wee Winnie Woolen that she wasn't going to be snatched from my back, kidnapped, and molested. I tried giving this dress to Pootie but she wouldn't take it.

This left Bessie Black. She'd gone to college with me

and remained loyal through thick and thin. She seemed to grow at the same rate that I did. She simply wouldn't wear out. I couldn't outgrow her or sell her at a rummage sale; the local thrift shop sent her back three times. Bessie Black was determined to march in my closet until doomsday. Although she'd cost only $16.95, she wore like cast iron. Once in a while she sprouted something that looked like mulch around her collar, but I just sponged her with a wet cloth and she perked right up. Lee was very partial to Bessie Black.

Not to be left out, the children named *their* clothing too. Lee shook his head, said we were *all* crazy, and continued to remind us all that, thank God, *he* was still sane enough to regard a shirt as a shirt as a shirt—and, by the way, where was his good white one with the blue dots and torn pocket?

"Oh, you mean Little Billy Blue Dot," I smiled sweetly. "You can wear him tonight because I washed him yesterday; he should be hanging somewhere between Scotty Sports Coat and Tommy Tweed Trousers."

"That reminds me, Mother," Karen said. "I can't find Fanny Fashion-Jeans."

Lee groaned.

"Should call those Tillie-Tightbutt," John snorted.

David doubled over happily at his brother's quick wit.

"At least," Karen sneered at her brothers, "I'm not required to call my tennis shoes Sammy Stink. If you don't stop, I'll tell Mother what you two call your jockey shorts when she isn't around."

"That's enough," I said. "You know the rule about fighting when we're having company." The rule plainly stated no fighting before, during, or after company. They knew that. We were entertaining a Navy buddy of Lee's and his new wife, whom we'd never met. We weren't even sure if she was number three or number four; but Lee insisted quantity wasn't important, it was the quality that mattered. "Bill always did have a good eye for the girls," he'd said. And since Lee had been stuck with the same one for so long, I thought I should try and make as good an impression as possible.

"Are you wearing Old Blue?" Susan asked with a turned-up nose. When I told her, no, I'd planned on Wrinkled Rear, she said that wasn't much better; she hoped the people who were coming weren't rich.

"Do they have any kids?" Amy asked.

Heavens, I certainly hoped not. They were still on their honeymoon. Amy seemed disappointed until I told her that she—along with John, David, Mary, and Claudia—was eating at Grandma's and staying overnight. We were keeping Karen and Susan home "to be the kitchen help since Dad won't hire a maid"; but the cold truth was Grandma said she could no longer handle all seven at the same time.

Smoothing Brown Wrinkled Rear carefully over my hips, I opened the door to Sailor Bill and his bride, whom he introduced with passionate fondness as Allison. I tried not to notice his hand down the front of her dress. Between the back slapping and handshaking of the two men, I took a gander at the little bride, a ravishing brunette. Sailor Bill made sure to point out that she definitely wasn't the same woman he'd had with him the last time we were together. "Got me a new model," and he slung two beefy arms across Lee's bent back, wisely observing, "But I see you have the same old girl, Good Buddy." Allison batted large blue-black eyes and shimmied her thighs against Good Buddy until his chin quivered and Little Billy nearly lost his dots.

"Take our guests' coats, please, girls," I instructed Karen and Susan, who were so busy trying to get close enough to Allison to see if such white teeth could be real that they'd forgotten their manners. A smart woman would've insisted Allison keep her coat *on* throughout the entire evening. She was wearing a deep-red velvet, cut to the kneecap, with tiny glittery thingamabobs sprinkled over the surface of the nap. Boy, did I have a name for *that* dress. Twittering like a bluejay, Lee said something dumb about how she lit up the house like the stars light up the night. The most romantic thing he'd ever said to me was "pass the mashed potatoes." Allison returned the compliment by shivering just enough to cause her "stars" to twinkle and, taking one look at Brown Wrinkled Rear, she put a diamond-dripping hand to her lips and said, "How sweet you look."

I handed her a tray of hot hors d'oeuvres and growled, "Take two. They are terribly fattening." Naturally, she turned them down (don't they always?) and I ate hers and mine and started on the ones I'd left in the kitchen and Lee grabbed my arm and said something about watching what I ate or I'd spoil my appetite. My appetite had started going on the fritz the minute Allison fluttered in the door, I told him.

"Can I help you with anything?" she gestured piteously and then flew over to sit so close to *my* husband that his knees took on a red cast from the rays of her dress. Sailor Bill was sloshing about in our best Scotch, pretending to be virile. I, the wrinkled brown crone who looked as if she'd been rolled up in a paper sack for twenty-four hours, was expected to wait on them all.

I was getting nowhere by being the perfect hostess. I might as well have been a calendar hanging on the wall. Therefore, in self-defense, when Lee left the room to get more ice, I looked Allison square in the eye, nudged the drunken sailor in his manly stomach, and told them I was very sorry the roast was cold but I'd been busy in the basement tucking away the remains of last night's dinner guests. "I often use my scissors on people who outstay their welcome, you know," I said casually.

"Good for yoush," wobbled the Navy, and Allison looked quite nervous.

Nervous changed to plain scared when Susan appeared in the doorway, wearing her nightgown (nicknamed Gay Gown until Karen took her aside and explained; from then on we called it Gertie or simply Nightgown) and insisting that I come right away and sew up poor Gertie. "She ripped real bad, Mom." Susan spread her hands for emphasis. I knew she meant her nightgown, and she knew she meant her nightgown, but Miss Pretty didn't. She hauled Sailor Bill to his feet, said it was time to go, nodded a quick good-bye to a surprised Lee, and left without even saying thank you.

Finally, by golly, I had gotten her attention.

It took about three days for Lee to stop giving me dirty looks because I'd scared Allison away before he'd had the opportunity to count every star on her planet.

33
Hot Tubs Are Not Much Fun Either

ONE NIGHT WHEN we were doing what we did about 95 percent of the time—eating—Amy, glancing around our bulging family table, leaned her pretty chin on chubby hands, looked me straight in the eye, and said, "Mommy, how come you have so many kids?"

"I ate a lot of peanut butter," I told her.

Karen choked on her spaghetti and quickly left the table to shove the Skippy jar to the darkest corner of the cupboard. "I'll not eat that again," she said with great conviction.

"I don't believe that, Mom," John broke in. "Peanut butter doesn't generate genes . . . only calories. Besides, Dad and I had a talk. I know what happened and it wasn't peanut butter."

"A lot you know," David interrupted. "I think Mom's right. When our mother hamster has babies, our science teacher puts peanut butter in her cage so she won't eat them. It must work because the hamster has about as many kids as we do."

I wasn't prone to gobbling up my babies when they were born. However, during certain periods of my life I truly was overwhelmed with an unusual craving for peanut butter. "How romantic can you get?" Lee had said, puzzled, when I dug out a box of crackers, a knife,

239

and a large jar of peanut butter, intending to feast upon our honeymoon bed. He had champagne in a bucket and caviar on the side. Cracker crumbs weren't exactly what he had in mind. Snuggling close, I explained that sometimes peanut butter turned me on; and since that day he's personally seen to it that the jar is never empty. Perhaps we've run out of salt, sugar, or soap over the years, but we've never run out of peanut butter. I've even seen him go out in a blizzard to get it, and he never, never complained of crumbs.

Following Mary's birth, my mother shook her head, and I caught her trying to sneak my jar of peanut butter out in her handbag. "This stuff is like poison to you," she said and left in a huff.

I wasn't hysterically happy about being turned into a sensual kitten by peanut butter, but at least I had enough sense not to order it in a public restaurant. "You don't know what it does to me," I told Helen one day while we were lunching downtown. She was nibbling a fresh peanut-butter-and-lettuce sandwich while I went through a chicken on rye. "For some reason it turns me into a seductress."

"Well, I can hardly believe that," Helen said coolly.

"It's true," I insisted. "Add a little lettuce or a banana, and I'm game for almost anything."

"You're possessed," she said and excused herself to go to the restroom to splash cold water on her face.

While she was gone, I coveted her sandwich. The more I looked, the more I wanted it. "Surely a tiny bite won't hurt." Reaching across the table, I sank my teeth into its peanuty softness. One swallow, and I felt the fingers of a fancy woman clutching my insides like a vise.

"Hi, there," I crooned to an ordinary, down-to-earth gentleman who'd wandered into the darkened dining room expecting to lunch with friends. Startled, he politely nodded in my direction, trying to ignore the peanut-butter sandwich I clutched.

"Good weather for winter wheat, isn't it?" I batted my eyes.

"I wouldn't know, ma'am, I sell shoes." Evidently he'd sold himself some very fast shoes, for he broke into such a run that he flew like a kite over the restaurant floor.

When Helen returned she crossed her arms, stood over my chair, and announced grumpily, "You've been eating my sandwich."

"How did you know that?"

"You have lettuce sticking out of your teeth!" So that was it, I thought. That was why the man had left so quickly. It wasn't me at all, it was the lettuce. No one could look like a sex symbol with green teeth.

After many years, my addiction to peanut butter became commonplace; no out-of-the-ordinary sensations sprouted as I munched. I switched to crunchy to see if I could rekindle new sparks, but all I ended up with was heartburn.

"We've changed," I told Lee as he slept in front of the television. "I can remember when our life wasn't quite so routine."

"So can I," he yawned.

"Maybe we've been married too long." Unlocking my knee joints as he sleepily reached out to help me to my feet, I made my way into the kitchen.

"Want a snack?" Lee asked, following.

"Sounds all right. What do you want?"

"Peanut butter," he snapped. God, the man just didn't know when to quit. And, boy, was I glad about that. I thought of poor Helen stuck with Ray and that ugly satin kimono and knew that, all told, I was a pretty lucky lady to have a husband like Lee to share with—even if it was only peanut butter.

After realizing that the peanut butter wasn't working quite as well as it should, we decided we had to get away, if only for a weekend, to forget we were parents, forget the utility bills, the sewer backup in the basement, tiresome telephone calls, and the fact that we had a dog always one step away from permanent incarceration in the city pound.

Naturally the children couldn't understand why we'd want to leave them, even for a minute; but, once in a while, Lee and I simply had to take a turn at being adults. We wanted a chance to go somewhere without having to rush around to find shoes. What a pleasure to enjoy a cocktail out of a glass that hadn't spent its first year of life as a jelly jar; how heavenly to be in an atmosphere where no one quarreled. This was the thing that bothered Lee the most. I let it run around me like the ticking of a clock; but because he was by nature a gentle man, he couldn't understand why they always seemed on the verge of scratching each other's eyes out. I tried explaining that the only brothers and sisters who didn't fuss and fight were, in reality, paper dolls or little Hummel figurines. I also warned him to start expecting more of it with the Christmas holidays around the corner, because they'd all be tensed up and under a strain trying to find the presents we'd hidden, if indeed we had hidden any. Lee always kept us in suspense by announcing in late November that *this* year there would probably be no more than a dollar and a quarter to spend on anyone.

"It will make us both feel better if we can get away for a weekend," I said. "I'll take along a little peanut butter and we can loll in the motel room and watch in-room movies that don't star collie dogs. We can each have our own bar of soap. It'll be fun. I promise." Valiant Grandma had noticed the pinched look around our eyes, forgot her pledge not to sit with all seven ever again, and volunteered to bring her nightgown and sleep over.

From the first minute I stepped into the motel, I had the funny feeling that maybe I should've stayed home. And after we'd registered and I'd checked out all the exits and fire extinguishers, Lee lured me into the swimming area with the promise of a tropical drink. We had changed into our bathing suits and I was decently covered in a muumuu and three sweaters. He was prancing by my side like a wild buck, and I wondered what the hell I was in for. Little did I know I was soon to be boiled alive.

I averted my eyes so I wouldn't have to see so much public nakedness as we passed the hot tub on our way to the bar. Lee, on the other hand, stood mesmerized.

"Would you look at that," he said, forgetting exotic drink and thirsty wife, as he watched a curvacious redhead, steam coming from her ears, wallowing around with four or five others in what seemed to be a big wooden barrel filled with boiling water. "Now that's something we have to try."

"Not I," I said. "What if they don't change the water?"

"It's practically the same thing as a swimming pool but more relaxing." He headed toward the wooden tub full of happy hot people. He couldn't fool me. I know a bathtub when I see one and I was convinced this type of recreation should be confined behind closed doors. "It's better than peanut butter," Lee called out as I marched back into our motel room to sit and sulk. When he returned about an hour later he was beet red and slapping his chest like Tarzan. "I feel twenty years younger," he said. "Finest thing I've done in months."

"Gee, thanks," I said, resisting the urge to tell him he looked like a boiled shrimp. Doing a few deep knee bends in front of the mirror to prove his newfound power, he told me I'd be sorry and stiff because I'd missed the experience. "And the people were so friendly and nice." I just bet they were, I thought, remembering the roasted redhead.

"Mark my words," I said, hoping to close the subject. "You'll catch your death of cold . . . or worse," and I purposely let my voice trail away so he could draw his own conclusions of just what kind of disease he might pick up in such a public place.

He laughed and said he planned to do it again the next day and probably the next. "I might even do it twice a day. Won't you even come and watch?"

"There's no need for me to do that," I said primly. "I'll just sit here in our motel room and try not to be lonely," and I hung my head pitifully.

"We could go late at night when no one else is around. No one will see you. You'll love it, I promise, and it will be an adventure. You keep complaining that your life is dull and that you wish you could have an adventure." I could see that it was either going to be Lassie and me alone in a motel room, or a hot tub and my husband. Reluctantly I consented to go, providing it was midnight and no one else was around. "Remember," I told him, "if there's one soul, I'm not getting in." Lee said I didn't have to.

Like a scared Cinderella I waited for the stroke of midnight. I drew the straps up on my bathing suit to a cutting tightness, put on a pair of tennis shoes, wrapped towels around my body, hair, and face, picked up my sweater, and said I was ready. "For what?" Lee chuckled, and in a huff I turned and ran into the wall.

"I can't see with this damn towel over my eyes," I said. "You'll have to help me," and he took my hand, guiding my path through the quiet motel halls and continuing to reassure me that everyone was fast asleep and we'd have the whole tub to ourselves. He kept saying over and over as I stumbled, blind as a bat, beside him, "You'll have fun. You'll have fun."

The hot tub seemed much less oppressive without people. A slight cloud of steam hovered over one corner and a lingering odor of damp wood and chlorine hung over the water like a blanket. "You'll have to leave the towels," Lee said, gently prying them from around my body, face, and hair. "And take off your shoes."

"You're not getting my bathing suit," I yelled, clutching the straps.

"I don't want it," he said much too quickly. Holding hands, we mounted the steps to the side of the hot tub together . . . Lee taking strong, determined steps and Shirley taking short, scared ones.

"Now," he said as we reached the top of the steps, "step in and sit down on the seat. That's all there is to it. Weren't you silly to be so afraid?"

"I'll get splinters."

"You won't get splinters." He jerked me inside the tub. Frankly, I found it to be very, very hot. I examined my body for signs of parboil as I decided that, so far, I wasn't having any fun.

"Close your eyes, lean back, and relax. Try to get used to it. I have a surprise for you," and he reached behind him to turn a lever placed on the wall. He was right. It was quite a surprise. He was trying to boil me alive. More hot water poured into the tub, only now it was churning and foaming about my body in fiery little bubbles. The hot tub had turned into a cauldron. All I needed to see was a group of painted wild people with spears dancing into the room. Never again would I nonchalantly toss potatoes into a boiling pot without an apology to each potato. It wouldn't have surprised me if a large hand had come from the sky and tossed in an onion or two.

"That's the bubbler," Lee said, pressing his head in pure bliss against the side of the tub. "Isn't this great? Just feel the smooth massage." I sat straight up in that tub and kept my eyes wide open and watched for blisters. "This is fun! This is fun!" I repeated over and over, trying to convince myself that being cooked was more fun than watching a collie on television.

We'd sat there for about four or five days (Lee said it was only ten minutes) when I heard the sound of strange voices coming into the area. I stood up, screamed, "My God, hide me" and took off out of the tub like a hot rocket, leaving behind towels, tennis shoes, sweater, and husband. My bare feet didn't even hit the corridor.

When I finally closed the door to our motel room safely behind me, I discovered my bathing suit had shrunk, my hands withered, my skin scorched. I had nightmares for two nights that I was being stirred and served as someone's supper. I certainly don't call that fun.

I should've stayed home and watched the children fight.

34
Christmas Is Coming— Tra La, Tra La

CHRISTMAS WAS A WONDERFUL time at our house if you didn't count Lee's set mouth, the overwrought children, and the fact that I had to buy a present for a dozen favorite teachers at $1.25 apiece. "I would like to buy my teacher *this*." Amy pointed to black peignoir with gaps like the Grand Canyon. It was featured in a fashion catalogue Karen had ordered from an advertisement in a movie magazine. The catalogue had arrived in a plain brown wrapper. Barely covering the model's deformed body, the nightie cost $79.50 plus asbestos wrapping and handling. Amy's teacher was middle-aged, sang in the church choir, and had a husband who, like mine, thought flannelette was racy. I persuaded Amy that a box of pretty soap would be more appropriate and then put the magazine out for Lee to see just in case he had $79.50 that he didn't know what to do with.

I loved this tinkling holiday with all my heart. Lee told me I didn't have to feel personally responsible for seeing that everyone in America had a gift to open on Christmas Eve, but with the first December snowfall, the first peal of "Jingle Bells" on the television, the first Christmas card in our mailbox, my metabolism churned and I hit the stores. Oh, there were so many pretty things to see and to handle and to buy. I loved giving. I didn't mind receiving either.

I didn't count the slaughtered masses of sweaters and mittens I'd knitted with passionate fervor as *real* Christmas presents (nor did the children); I felt it was very important that each child find at least one special asked-for gift under the tree.

Thank God, Lee agreed. "Within reason, of course," he said.

This ruled out seventy-nine-dollar nightgowns, individual color television sets, Hondas, and Bo Derek. Karen wanted us to add a wing to the house so she could have her own apartment. "Remember," I said, "Dad said within reason." Busy as bees, they presented us with their final lists—reasonable things like fashion boots, model airplanes, dolls, and stuffed toys. "We can handle this," Lee promised with a warm Christmas feeling. I scanned the newspaper ads for the best prices and for three hours marked, checked, and circled the stores I would go to first. But because it's always been my lot in life never to be in the right place at the right time, I proudly purchased a pair of roller skates for Susan at a marvelous price of $22.50 on Friday only to have the exact pair pop up in the paper for $9 and double trading stamps on Saturday. I told myself it was Christmas, sluffed it off, and tried not to let it bother me. I also tried not to let Lee see the paper.

This was the year we found the spirit of Christmas walking the floor of a large department store in the form of a very special person. He wasn't wearing a red suit; nor did he have a white beard. He was dressed in a slightly buckled beige jacket and had tired eyes. We were reaching the end of our shopping list, with all major gifts purchased except Mary's request. She wanted one thing from Santa. One precious thing.

"A Gaylord, Mommy, I want a Gaylord." For six weeks a mechanical brown-and-white beagle dog with floppy ears and big feet had walked across the television

screen to fetch a bone. Because Mary cared little for batteries, plastic, or joints made moveable by rubber bands,
to her Gaylord was a marvel. A doggie just her size. One
on a leash that didn't pull her arms from their sockets
when he spied Amigo, the neighborhood harlot, leaning
on a lamppost. A doggie that could jump on her and not
knock her to the floor and that she could keep in her
room without fear of being gassed. "Please, Mommy, I
want a Gaylord so bad." Her blond curls danced in anticipation and blue eyes sparkled with pure love. At bedtime her prayer included, "God bless Mommy, Daddy,
Grandma, Grandpa, and Gaylord."

She would have her Gaylord, Lee declared. He took
the afternoon off from work to find one. There wasn't a
mechanical beagle in town. He'd looked and looked, he
said, coming home defeated. Gaylord had disappeared.
He continued to appear on television but was absolutely
invisible on store shelves. I was becoming paranoid and
Lee started offering substitutes.

"See the doll," he bribed Mary. "She walks, talks,
rolls her eyes, cries, and wets her panties."

"Claudia does all that," Mary said, crawling up on
his lap. "I'll play with her. I want a Gaylord, all my
own."

Lee flipped the pages of a toy catalogue. "I see a
pretty set of dishes here."

"Gaylord has his own dish," she said happily. "Just
like Augie, only he doesn't throw up in it. And he has
his very own bone that doesn't stink." She stroked her
daddy's cheek with little-girl confidence.

"Oh, see here," Lee said enthusiastically. "An organ.
Just your size. One that plays real music. Wouldn't you
like your own organ?" Mary kissed him soundly on the
lips and said "Nope! I don't want an organ." I do, I felt
like saying. I'd always wanted an organ.

After Mary had raced to her room to once again

straighten the bright blue quilted coverlet she'd borrowed from Amy's doll so Gaylord would have a nice bed all ready when he arrived on Christmas morning, Lee turned to me and shook his head. "What are we going to do? We have to find that silly dog."

Feelers went out to family and friends. "If you spot a Gaylord, let us know." No one did, until Helen came over with a newspaper ad that featured this magical dog for only $8. At that point we would've paid $800. "It isn't good to give in to little children," she said. Since Lee considered Helen a poop about 90 percent of the time, this made him more determined than ever to buy Gaylord. The two of us rushed out the door, leaving an astonished Helen with the children.

When we arrived at the store I searched through the toy section, giftware, appliances, and canned goods. No Gaylord. "He's gone." I clutched Lee's arm. "Gaylord is gone. I can't find him anywhere." So close and I'd missed him. Grabbing a floorwalker by the sleeve, I shouted into his ear, "Where's Gaylord?"

"Lord, lady, I don't know. We've lost two hundred little kids in the past three hours. Did you look in Customer Service?"

"Gaylord isn't my child. He's a dog. A toy dog. You advertised."

"Oh, *that* Gaylord. He's sold out. Went like hotcakes." As he started to turn away, I crumpled right there in the aisle. "I have to have a Gaylord," I sobbed.

"I'm sorry he's gone." His face softened. "I can special-order one, but I'm afraid he won't be here for Christmas." I couldn't hold back the disappointed tears that ran down my cheeks as I stood in the middle of that bustling department store. As the carts bumped around me and people stared, the strains of "Little Drummer Boy" sounded over the loudspeaker. I wondered, where was my Christmas miracle?

"It's all our little girl asked for," I wept. "And we can't give it to her."

"Just a minute," the salesman said quietly. "I think I can help you." For some reason he didn't look so tired anymore. "I put one of those dogs back for my niece. I'll let you have it. I'll buy her a little organ. Lord knows we have plenty of those left." He went and returned to place Gaylord in my arms.

I kissed that dog. I also kissed my husband, two startled passersby, and would've kissed the salesman, but he'd disappeared into a crowd of shoppers. "I didn't even get to properly thank him," I told Lee as we drove home in the lovely Christmasy falling snow, Gaylord carefully cuddled between us.

"Somehow, in some way, I think he knows," Lee said softly.

35

Santa Blows His Cool

OUR CHILDREN COULD hardly stand the suspense of Christmas. John always ran a temperature. David broke out in little red spots and was often constipated. Karen and Susan could handle it no longer and finally relieved *their* suspense by unwrapping and rewrapping everyone's presents a dozen times. Mary, Amy, and Claudia still believed in Santa and thought all the gifts we'd been buying were for the poor kids in India who liked liver and green beans. Hearing suddenly became razor sharp. Though everyone seemed cotton-eared when the word went out to come fold your laundry, the rustle of a piece of wrapping paper during December would immediately bring someone to my elbow.

"What are you wrapping, Mom?" John asked breathlessly.

"I thought you were at Gary's house." Gary lived three blocks away.

"Oh, I was," he said. "But I thought I heard this noise at home, and if we had prowlers, I figured you'd need my help. I got here as fast as I could." The child had become a Yuletide Bionic.

During the Christmas season Lee and I didn't dare speak in our native tongue. Because neither of us were psychic, we held secret meetings to discuss the Christmas list. Huddled under our covers at night, while other married couples kissed and hugged, we thumbed through the Sears catalogue.

"Here's something David needs," I whispered. "It's a set of mathematical flash cards."

"David doesn't want that, Mom," a soft little voice came from the foot of our bed. "David would rather have a soccer ball."

"How did he get in here?" Lee said in a startled voice. "I thought I had the door locked." I thought of the other times we'd had the door locked but shook that out of my head and told him locked doors meant nothing to children at Christmastime. I started setting the alarm clock for 5 A.M. "That should fool them," I said confidently. "It's a schoolday and they never get up early on a schoolday." Lee grumbled something about not getting up this early either. "I'll meet you at the coffeepot," I said. "With the catalogue." Wide awake, Lee's Christmas spirit was weak but when he was sleepy it was downright puny. He promised to join me as soon as he did something about the bags under his eyes. The house was very, very quiet at 5 A.M. Outside it was dark and cold. I knew we'd get an awful lot done in such a peaceful atmosphere. Lee's head was nodding over the toaster but I was sure I'd get his attention the minute I got to the $350 stereo outfits. I'd bet my last Christmas cookie that he'd wake up then. I carefully and quietly turned the first page of the catalogue. It was like the shot heard around the world. Feet pounded down the stairs, a cheerful "Good morning, Mommy, good morning, Daddy, what are you doing?" split the air. Augie barked, the cat jumped up and down, the ice maker clicked on . . . the whole damn house was wide awake. All but Lee. He was sleeping with his nose in the butter.

We didn't make one gift selection that morning, so that evening I tried pig latin. I'd learned it from my

older sisters, who had communicated this way all
through high school—baffling my father, confusing my
mother, driving boyfriends mad, and guaranteeing me a
few stray dimes when I promised not to tell what I'd
interpreted. It had yielded a good bit of pocket money
and I'd developed a fluency of my own. I could do
twenty-minute conversations without pausing. Lee
couldn't understand a word I said.

"Ott-way ooo-day oo-yay ink-thay abay-outbay i-bay-
ickel-says or-fay uh-they oise-bays?" I rattled casually
while I passed him a piece of white cake. His brow
wrinkled and his brain worked. He didn't dare answer
yes until he'd figured out what I said. For all he knew I
might be asking for a mink coat or a microwave.

Before I could repeat it slowly and throw in a hint or
two, John had slammed down four color brochures and
six bicycle sales pitches on the advantages of ten speeds
over three speeds. So I scrapped pig latin and started
writing notes for Lee. I put them in places I didn't think
even our curious children would look, but Lee complained that it was uncomfortable sitting around the office all day with tiny pieces of paper taped to his shorts
that reminded him "to pick up Barbie doll on sale at
drugstore." I turned to spelling around the two little
girls and discovered that although Claudia couldn't
master d-o-g, or c-a-t, she knew every letter in Mattel,
Kenner, and Fisher-Price. And if medical science can
come up with the answer to why five-year-olds suddenly
sprout angel wings during the Christmas season, I wish
they'd write me a letter. Amy tippy-toed around the
house and was so quiet and good that I became worried.
She refused to sit near the dining-room window during
the first twenty-four days of December; her brother John
had told her Santa Claus was peeking through the curtains and would see her feed Mom's best stew to the cat.
"He has his eye on you, girlie," John said. Amy ran to

me and buried her face in my lap. "I'll eat my stew, Mommy, from now on. The kitty didn't like it anyway."

I was also under the assumption that all small children would immediately take to Santa Claus. I never considered the possibility that Claudia, who often reacted in unholy terror when a beloved grandmother entered the room wearing a new pair of eyeglasses, wouldn't immediately nestle up to a strange Santa.

"I'm planning to have the children's pictures taken with Santa," I told Lee one Monday evening about ten days before Christmas. He'd just crunched through the door exclaiming that the icy roads were murder and he hoped he wouldn't have to leave the house again until spring. "The mall is running a special tonight."

"You really don't expect me to go along, do you?" he said. I certainly did. Why should he miss such a darling experience because of a little ice and snow? Karen and Susan begged off by claiming a headache; the two boys said they wouldn't be caught dead having their pictures taken with Santa Claus; Mary had a cold; and Amy had eaten so much stew that she couldn't be taken more than six inches from the nearest bathroom. This left Claudia, who smiled for pictures only when her daddy stood on his head in the corner of the living room. She wasn't ordinarily bad-tempered—just humorless and very suspicious of anyone holding a camera.

Karen said she'd watch over things at home if I'd give her written permission to bump off the boys if they gave her one second's problems. I left Grandma's number in case of an emergency, promised the boys they could each have two doughnuts for breakfast for the rest of the week if they'd be good, told Susan to stay off the telephone in case I needed to call home, gave Mary a cough drop and Amy a sturdy dose of nasty brown-tasting medicine and a cough drop because she wanted one. I dressed Claudia in the prettiest velvety outfit she owned, put a ribbon in her hair and clean stockings on her feet. She thought we were going to church.

"Sunday school?" she asked in a puzzled manner. Two days in a row seemed a bit much, but she was willing as she liked her teacher and they served cookies. "No, dear," I smiled. "We're going to see Santa and have your picture taken." Santa ... Sunday school ... so what? She shrugged her little shoulders. For all she knew, he'd have some cookies too.

It was growing late when we finally reached the mall, and Lee found a parking place and ranted for twenty minutes about why every dumb so-and-so in town had to go out shopping on a night like this. He was in a rotten mood. So were Santa and his photographer. Obviously, they'd been at it for a long, long time. The photographer resembled a man who'd just been informed that his brand-new automobile had been towed away and dumped in the icy depths of the Platte River; Santa lethargically jingled his sleigh bells with a numb elbow. "What have we here?" he rasped, as we brought Claudia close to his big throne in the center of the mall.

"A little girl who wants her picture taken with Santa," I coyly simpered. Claudia buried her head in her daddy's shoulder and screamed bloody murder.

"Come sit on Santa's lap," I coaxed.

"No!" she cried.

"Will you smile for the nice man?"

"No!" she sobbed louder.

"Will you open your eyes?"

"No!" A lot of people had stopped to watch.

"Boo!" yelled the photographer.

"Well, you don't have to frighten her to death," I scolded. "I can assure you that you'll get nowhere by yelling. Maybe her daddy will stand on his head in the corner."

"Her daddy will *not* stand on his head in the corner,"

Lee growled. The crowd looked quite disappointed. Santa, eyes lighting up and saliva appearing at the corner of his mouth, spied a young lady in a fishnet sweater and tight jeans who was swiveling up to the front of the crowd standing around. "Ho, ho, ho!" he chuckled, stretching out two mittened hands toward the sweet young thing.

"No, no, no!" slammed her six-foot-four boyfriend, who had materialized from behind the Christmas tree.

"Pay attention to business, Claus," the photographer snapped, "or we'll never get home. Give the kid some candy and let's get on with it." Santa puffed once and rumbled around in his sack for a candy cane and waved it in front of Claudia. Forgetting her fear, she suddenly jumped from Lee's arms and straight into Santa's and, taking the candy from him, put it right into her mouth. Claudia took six strong licks and entwined ten sticky fingers in Santa's beard, poking the tip of the candy cane into his nose. Santa, forgetting where he was and *who* he was, yelled, "Holy Mother of God!" and stood up in his chair, scattering the waiting line of children like chickens.

"I think you'd better stand on your head. Quick!" I told Lee.

Without warning, Claudia did an about-face. Reaching up, she touched Santa gently on the cheek; then, bending over in childish innocence, she simply kissed his mittened hand. "I love you, little Santa Claus," she whispered. Like magic, the camera clicked. The picture was taken and it was one of the best I've ever seen.

If you look really, really close you can see a tiny tear in the corner of Santa's eye.

36
A Letter to Santa Claus

GOSH, IT'S THAT TIME AGAIN. How have you been? I'm sorry I haven't written for so long. Probably it's been thirty years or so since you heard from me. The last time I wrote I asked for a tiny baby and you eventually brought seven. Gee, thanks, Santa, you're a real sport. But this year, if you don't mind, I'd rather have a can opener.

Why am I writing after so much time? Oh, I don't know. Sometimes I feel like keeping in touch with old friends and old memories. Isn't that what Christmas is all about? I suppose you're sitting there with smoke circling your head like a wreath wondering when I'm going to get around to asking for presents. Don't worry, I will. But first I'd like a little advice. You see, Santa, I have this husband—his name is Lee—and he's really a nice guy and all, but every year we have a fight over the Christmas tree. I want to go to the supermarket lot and buy one and he wants to go to this tree farm where we can get it free. I don't mind free; but, Santa, these are puny trees. If you're looking for ugly, you've got it.

For instance, here's what happened last year:

"Do you see what I see?" I shouted as we drove down the street in front of a parking lot full of dozens of lovely, straight, tall trees dangling for dollars right there for the picking.

"Listen to what I say!" he answered. "Anyone can *buy* a tree. We're going to have the unique opportunity to choose and cut our own." He's the only one in the car who wanted to make the trip.

Not even a star on top will help most of those trees, believe me. If I could persuade our guests to come in the door, say hello, and then lie down on their backs, I suppose the tree wouldn't look all that bad, but few people enjoy visiting, eating, and singing Christmas carols while flat on the floor. There's three feet between every branch and although he drills holes and fills in the spaces, it still looks like the tree has a terminal case of wilt. Maybe you've noticed. I bet you have. You've probably seen quite a few weird trees in your day. By the way, my neighbor Helen has the same problem with her husband, Ray. I talked to her yesterday and she had tears in her voice. She said she cried every year over their Christmas tree and kept the blinds drawn so no one could see in from the outside. She won't even let me come over for coffee. I told her it wasn't that important. A tree was only a tree and after all it's just once a year, but a husband hangs around the house 365 days. I have to admit I'm filled in sort of funny between the branches myself, and Lee continues to claim he finds beauty there. Who knows . . . maybe it's because I'm free.

I have a personal favor to ask, Santa. It doesn't have anything to do with Christmas but it means a lot to me. I have this problem at service stations. I don't mean the self-service kind, heavens, no, I can't work those. I'm scared to death of gasoline, so I always go to the ones marked "Full Service"—but I never get it. They fill the gas tank in fine order because I have a credit card, but it's my windshield that needs attention. It always seems to have three inches of mud, grit, and grime on it; but do you think it gets cleaned? Not on your life! They don't even flip a rag over it. But let a young blonde size nine pull in next to me, and she has men swarming all over her hood. She doesn't even have a gnat obstructing her view, and they spend fifteen minutes polishing. Don't bring them anything this year, Santa Claus. Not even a wrench.

And don't pay any attention to the ornaments hanging on the tree. I made those. Pretty awful, aren't they? They looked super in the magazine. They're called "Dough-Doobies" and it took me eight hours and twenty dollars' worth of ingredients to turn out fourteen of those little buggers that look like burned bread with dabs of paint globbed in the cracks. They're supposed to be angels, drums, and toy soldiers. I hid them in the closet. Lee laughed and said they'd draw mice. Serve them right!

Amy and Mary found them, said, "These are pretty, Mommy," and hung them on the tree one day when I wasn't looking, so I said what the heck and just left them there.

Now to get to my list. I really don't want too much. I hope you can bring me:

A telephone that self-destructs if it rings before 9 A.M. on Saturday morning

A key to a bank vault

An electric stocking stuffer

An electric flour duster for liver

Enough electricity to run them *and* five blow dryers all at the same time

Three whole days when I look just like Jane Fonda. Now, I'm not asking for a lifetime . . . just three days. I'd like to see what happens. I think three days will be long enough.

A lady to come in the day after Christmas to sort puzzle pieces and find Barbie-doll boots. A patient lady who doesn't scream, "They're your toys. How should *I* know!"

A friend (or enemy) who'd invite a large family over for Sunday dinner . . . or Tuesday supper . . . or Thursday lunch

A special silver star in Grandma's crown. She deserves it. I bet you think so too.

A sewing machine that says, "You go sit by the television set now, I'll finish this."

A size-nine figure

And, Santa, if you can't manage everything on my list, just bring the size-nine figure and the key to the bank vault. Everything else will fall into place.

Well, I suppose I should close this. It's three days until Christmas and it's time I did something terrific to the house. Our family and friends will all be here and we'll be looking forward to you. I'll leave some milk and cookies under the tree—but if I were you, I wouldn't eat any angels, drums, or toy soldiers.

With love,
Shirley Lueth

37
A Christmas Fairy Tale

I STILL BELIEVE IN Santa Claus; don't you? I still believe that he's strong and able and has a bad temper sometimes, and once in a while he scolds his elves and reindeer and spouts off to Mrs. Claus, and that he stays late at the toy shop on occasion while the sugar plums burn on the kitchen stove and Mrs. Claus spews and fumes—and then when he comes in the door, all rosy and cold, stomping his feet on the floor, spraying snow all over, and says, "It's good to be home!" and he tosses kisses from the pack on his back to everyone around, pats Mrs. Claus on her round little bottom, everything is merry and bright because he's there and it is good.

Never mind that at times he drops off to sleep in the middle of someone's Christmas list. A signal, perhaps hidden beneath his beard, must go off because he never sleeps when it's important to be awake. So what that his sleigh has a dent in it, there's a hole in the toe of his sock, a button is missing from his red coat, and maybe the twinkle in his eyes dims now and then because he carries the weight of someone else's happiness on his shoulders and he doesn't quite know how he's going to make them smile again . . . but he does. And he sticks around. That's the important part of Santa Claus at our house. He sticks around. He doesn't just drop in once a year.

He says if he didn't stick around, who'd keep those elves in line? My goodness, if those little rascals had their way they'd goof off and wouldn't get a single thing done—and then where would we be? Knowing them, they'd wait until Christmas Eve to do the things they should've been doing in August.

Nothing suits an elf better than sleeping all morning and playing all night. They fight over the glue pot, spill paints, hide Santa's favorite pipe, steal Mrs. Claus's Christmas cookies and cakes, call fairies on the telephone, tease the reindeer, play music boxes until they squeak, turn somersaults on the stars, and complain about having to wear the same old pointed shoes and green jackets they wore last year. They beg to borrow Santa's sleigh and Santa sighs and lets them have it and doesn't get too upset when they pile it in a snowdrift or get low on runner wax. Occasionally the elves leave the North Pole in a tiff because Santa's old-fashioned and no one believes in him anymore anyway, least of all them—and then they get out in the world and discover Silent Night means just that . . . especially when they are all alone.

"It's nice to know," they say, when they become major elves and have collected a little common sense, "that Santa's house is open three hundred sixty-five days and that he never takes a day off from love."

As for the reindeer, no home should be without one. Santa threatens to call the animal angels when a hoof plunges through a special toy drum, or funny business goes on in the corner of the workshop or the reindeer licks the hand of the Grinch that would steal Christmas instead of biting it like a good reindeer would. The elves put up a hue and cry and unanimously agree to feed and water him, keep his antlers clean, and see that he takes to the woods for his daily devotions; they promise Santa that if he'll keep him one more year, Santa won't have to lift a hand. Santa knows that it probably won't happen but goes along with it anyway and the reindeer stays, at least for now. True, his nose doesn't light up but his tail wags in real Christmas spirit.

And it wouldn't seem like Christmas without Mrs. Santa Claus, not at our house or yours. She hustles Santa, nags the elves, shakes a finger at the reindeer, and still carries a sign on her back that proclaims, "Peace on earth. Good will toward men," and you'd better not forget it, brother, not for a minute. She has the responsibility for cookies, candy, hams, yams, and fruit cake, establishing a worldwide reputation and tradition for sour divinity.

Her pfeffernüsse has too much pfeffer and not enough nüsse; and assorted gingerbread men, wearing funny clothes, prance about the cottage looking and acting as if they've been sampling the cooking sherry. She smiles, lays a finger beside her nose, and says, "I love you, Big Red," and Santa doesn't know if she means him or the Nebraska Cornhusker football team. And she won't tell.

She can be seen peering in a jewelry-store window around the North Pole square, looking wistfully at diamonds and being happy with a deep-fat fryer because of the spirit in which it is given. She stretches each Christmas dollar a mile, fills the elves' stockings with secrets, smiles, and mutilated sweaters, sings carols off-key, and can be caught sitting up in the middle of the night, alone, looking out the window with a tear on her cheek, watching for the star in the east and wondering if swaddling clothes are warm enough for a baby in a manger.

You see, Christmas lives at our house every day. I bet it does at yours, too!

B.8